Intro to Science
Teacher Guide

> # THIS PRODUCT IS INTENDED FOR HOME USE ONLY
>
> The images and all other content in this book are copyrighted material owned by Elemental Science, Inc. Please do not reproduce this content on e-mail lists or websites. If you have an eBook, you may print out as many copies as you need for use WITHIN YOUR IMMEDIATE FAMILY ONLY. Duplicating this book or printing the eBook so that the book can then be reused or resold is a violation of copyright.
>
> **Schools and co-ops:** You MAY NOT DUPLICATE OR PRINT any portion of this book for use in the classroom. Please contact us for licensing options at support@elementalscience.com.

Intro to Science Teacher Guide

Updated Edition, 2018 (Second Printing, 2020)
Copyright @ Elemental Science, Inc.

ISBN # 978-1-935614-66-1

Printed in the USA for worldwide distribution

For more copies write to:
Elemental Science
PO Box 79
Niceville, FL 32588
support@elementalscience.com

Copyright Policy

All contents copyright © 2020, 2018, 2011 by Elemental Science. All rights reserved.

Limit of Liability and Disclaimer of Warranty: The publisher has used its best efforts in preparing this book, and the information provided herein is provided "as is." Elemental Science makes no representation or warranties with respect to the accuracy or completeness of the contents of this book and specifically disclaims any implied warranties of merchantability or fitness for any particular purpose and shall in no event be liable for any loss of profit or any other commercial damage, including but not limited to special, incidental, consequential, or other damages.

Trademarks: This book identifies product names and services known to be trademarks, registered trademarks, or service marks of their respective holders. They are used throughout this book in an editorial fashion only. In addition, terms suspected of being trademarks, registered trademarks, or service marks have been appropriately capitalized, although Elemental Science cannot attest to the accuracy of this information. Use of a term in this book should not be regarded as affecting the validity of any trademark, registered trademark, or service mark. Elemental Science is not associated with any product or vendor mentioned in this book.

Table of Contents

Introduction 5

Required Book List 10

Optional Library Book List 10

Unit 1: Intro to Chemistry 17

Unit Overview	18
Solids and Liquids ~ Week 1	20
Solutions ~ Week 2	24
Density ~ Week 3	28
Crystals ~ Week 4	32
Colors ~ Week 5	36
Freezing ~ Week 6	40

Unit 2: Intro to Physics 45

Unit Overview	46
Gravity ~ Week 1	48
Magnets ~ Week 2	52
Inclined Planes ~ Week 3	56
Static Electricity ~ Week 4	60
Pulleys ~ Week 5	64
Light ~ Week 6	68

Unit 3: Intro to Geology 73

Unit Overview	74
Fossils ~ Week 1	76
Rocks ~ Week 2	80
Metamorphic Rock ~ Week 3	84
Volcano ~ Week 4	88
Sedimentary Rock ~ Week 5	92
Compass ~ Week 6	96

Unit 4: Intro to Meteorology 101

Unit Overview	102

The Sun ~ Week 1	104
The Water Cycle ~ Week 2	108
The Seasons ~ Week 3	112
Wind ~ Week 4	116
Tornadoes ~ Week 5	120
Thermometer ~ Week 6	124

Unit 5: Intro to Botany 129

Unit Overview	130
Plants ~ Week 1	132
Flowers ~ Week 2	136
Seeds ~ Week 3	140
Leaves ~ Week 4	144
Stems ~ Week 5	148
Roots ~ Week 6	152

Unit 6: Intro to Zoology 157

Intro to Zoology Unit Overview	158
Fish ~ Week 1	160
Butterflies ~ Week 2	164
Invertebrates ~ Week 3	168
Mammals ~ Week 4	172
Reptiles ~ Week 5	176
Birds ~ Week 6	180

Appendix 185

Rock Candy Recipe	187
The Water Cycle	188
Parts of a Flower	189
Parts of a Seed	190
Butterfly Life Cycle Pictures	191
Chicken Skeleton	192
Narration Sheet Template	194
Project Sheet Template	195
Scheduling Templates	196

Intro to Science – Introduction

Intro to Science has been written to give you the tools you need to gently introduce the students to the world of science. They will work on increasing their observation skills as they learn different topics within the major disciplines of science. This program lays out thirty-six weekly topics to study, along with a main idea to emphasize. Each week includes a scripted introduction, two hands-on projects, additional library book suggestions, and activities. Intro to Science is designed to be used with five- to seven-year-old students.

Why teach science to preschoolers?

The preschool student is learning daily about their environment. They are constantly taking in information about the world around them through hands-on experiences. They enjoy seeing how things work and love being introduced to new things. The preschooler is more than ready and willing to learn, but their motor muscles aren't quite ready for all the writing that formal education entails.

Typically preschoolers are taught the basics, such as colors, letters, and numbers, through simple worksheets. We also provide them with structured play, such as a kitchen set or a dress up station. We make sure that they have time to build their motor skills through creating art and exploring music.

However, all too often, we neglect to introduce our youngest students to the wonder of science because we think it is too difficult a subject for them to grasp. While some concepts in science will go way over a preschooler's head, we can introduce them to the subject as a whole by presenting them with the way that things work in their environment.

Preschoolers are naturally wired to be curious; thus, they are fully prepared to learn about science. These early years are a good time to introduce them to how things work in their environment because an early introduction to the subject will create an interest that you can build upon once they reach the elementary years. By showing them the miracle of the scientific processes going on around them, you are constructing a basis for future learning.

In *Success in Science: A Manual for Excellence in Science Education*, we state that the goal for preschool science is simply to introduce your students to the world around them. It is with this goal in mind that we have written *Intro to Science*. This year, your students will be exploring the wonderful world of science through a buffet of weekly topics, hands-on projects, books, and activities. All this will work together to build a basic framework, or bucket, the students can fill with information during the elementary years.

Let's take a closer look at the sections in this guide.

The Weekly Topic

The main purpose of having a weekly topic is to create a focus for your studies for the week. Each week, this section will provided the main idea for the week, along with a scripted introduction. This introduction may contain simple explanations, brief demonstrations, and/or guided observations for you to use when introducing the students to the week's topic.

As part of the this section, we have provided a pre-planned script for you to read, but feel free to use your own words or edit the script as you communicate the information. The main purpose of introducing the topic is to share with your students what they will be studying for the week. Your introduction should only take five to fifteen minutes because of the students' short attention spans.

After you introduce the week's topic (or during, if you have a fidgety student), you can have the students color the coordinating coloring page for their scrapbook.

Hands-on Projects

The hands-on projects in this guide include simple scientific demonstrations and nature studies. Scientific demonstrations are designed to help the students see the science of their environment in action, while nature studies are designed to aid the students in learning about the world around them through discovery and observation.

All the scientific demonstrations come from *More Mudpies to Magnets*. The goal of these hands-on projects is to demonstrate science for the students. Don't expect them to be able to predict the outcome or to draw abstract conclusions at this age. Instead, allow them to observe and tell what they have learned, no matter how simple it may seem to you. After you finish the demonstration, you can have the students fill out a demonstration sheet for their scrapbook.

The nature studies included in the hands-on project sections will also coordinate with the weekly topic. The purpose of these nature studies is to have the students learn about the world around them through discovery and observation. After you finish the nature study activity, you can have the students fill out a nature journal sheet for their scrapbook. Allow them to draw what they would like or glue a picture on the page instead. At this stage, it is best for you to write down their observations for them.

You can choose one or both of these hands-on projects in your weekly plan.

Read-Alouds

During the preschool years, students usually love to be read to, and science is a good topic to explore through books at this age. For this reason, we have included a list of optional library books for you to choose from each week. These books are suggestions that you can get from your local library. We have not previewed each and every book, so be sure to do so before you read them to the students.

Coordinating Activities

Coordinating activities are meant to reinforce what the student is learning in science. In this guide, we have included craft ideas, snack options, and additional projects that will tie into the weekly topic.

Optional Schedules

We have written *Intro to Science* as a topical study – each week stands alone, but the week also fits into a four week unit. This gives you, the teacher, complete freedom in deciding which order you want to do this study, how much you want to do in a week, and how many days you want to study science per week. Our goal is to allow you the opportunity to pick and choose activities that interest your students.

We would suggest scheduling science for two (20 minute) blocks a week or five (10 minute) blocks a week. As part of the lesson materials for each week, we have included two sample schedules to give you an idea of how you could schedule your time. You can choose to use these as your guide or create your own schedule using one of the blank scheduling templates in the Appendix on pp. 196-197 of this guide.

Student Materials

We offer two resources for the students to record what they have learned during this study – the Lapbooking Templates (LT) and the Student Diary (SD).

The Lapbooking Templates

The lapbooking templates included a set of templates for six lapbooks to go along with this program. Each lapbook has six mini-books, one for each weekly topic, a project folder template, and a color cover for the lapbook. We have included a pre-written main idea sentence to paste into each mini-book or you can have the students copy the main idea sentence into the mini-book.

The Student Diary

The student diary pages are simple journal sheets where the students record what they have learned and done over the year. They include coloring pages, demonstration sheets, activity pages, and nature journal sheets to use each week. The following is a description of how the individual scrapbook pages are designed to be used:

- Coloring Page – Read the main idea at the bottom of the page to the students as you have them color the picture.
- Demonstration Sheet – Have the students tell you what they learned from the scientific demonstration and write it down for them on the lines provided. Include any applicable pictures in the boxes provided.
- Activity Page – Have your students draw a picture or paste in a picture of the craft project they made on the sheet provided.
- Nature Journal Sheet – Have the students tell you what they learned from the nature study activity and write it down for them on the lines provided. Include any applicable pictures in the boxes provided.

Please visit the following website to see both of the options for your students:

http://elementalscience.com/collections/intro-to-science

How to include an older student

If you want an older student to do this study along with the younger students, here are some suggestions to increase the difficulty of this program so that it is more appropriate for them.

1. Have the older students read the additional books to the younger students.
2. Have the older students read more about the weekly topic in the *Usborne First Encyclopedia of Science* or the *Usborne Internet-linked Science Encyclopedia*.
3. Have the older students write full narrations as well as do a more detailed write-up for the demonstrations using the template pages included in the Appendix on pp. 194.

Helpful Articles

Our goal as a company is to provide you with the information you need to be successful in your quest to educate your students in the sciences at home. This is the main reason we share tips and tools for homeschool science education as blogs. As you prepare to guide your students through this program, you may find the following articles helpful:

- *Observation is Key* – This article explains the importance of observation, along with how nature study and scientific demonstrations can help you build the

students observation skills.
- http://elementalscience.com/blogs/news/63858627-observation-is-key
- ***Scientific Demonstrations vs. Experiments*** – This article shares about these two types of scientific tests and points out how to employ scientific demonstrations or experiments in your homeschool.
  - http://elementalscience.com/blogs/news/89905795-scientific-demonstrations-or-experiments
- ***What is nature study?*** – This article clarifies what nature study is and the basic components of this style of hands-on science activity.
  - http://elementalblogging.com/what-is-nature-study/

Additional Resources

The following page contains quick links to the activities suggested in this guide, along with several helpful downloads:

- https://elementalscience.com/blogs/resources/intro

Final Thoughts

As the author and publisher of this curriculum, I encourage you to contact us with any questions or problems that you might have concerning *Intro to Science* at support@elementalscience.com. We will be more than happy to answer them as soon as we are able. I hope that you enjoy *Intro to Science*!

Required Book List

The following book is scheduled for use in this guide. You will need to purchase it to be able to complete the scientific demonstrations and nature study.

- **{For the demonstrations}** *More Mudpies to Magnets : Science for Young Children* by Sherwood, Williams, and Rockwell (1990 edition)

- **{For the nature studies}** *The Handbook of Nature Study* by Anne Botsford Comstock (1986 edition)
(*Note – This book is more of a teacher reference than a book to read to your student. The idea is that you as the teacher will read the material ahead of time so that you will have the knowledge to assist your student as they learn through their own observations of nature. It is NOT designed to be read to the student.*)

The following encyclopedia is scheduled throughout the year when it contains a coordinating topic. It is completely optional! But, if you plan on using it, I recommend that you purchase it since you will use it for multiple weeks.

- *The Usborne Children's Encyclopedia* (2014 edition)

Optional Library Book List

Unit 1: Intro to Chemistry

Week 1
- *What is the world made of? All about solids, liquids and gases (Let's Read and Find out About Science)* by Kathleen Weidner Zoehfeld and Paul Meisel
- *Change It!: Solids, Liquids, Gases and You (Primary Physical Science)* by Adrienne Mason and Claudia Davila
- *Solids, Liquids and Gases (Starting with Science)* by Ray Boudreau

Week 2
- *Liquids* (States of Matter) by Carol Ryback and Jim Mezzanotte
- *Lulu's Lemonade* (Math Matters) by Barbara Derubertis and Paige Billin-Frye

Week 3
- *What Is Density?* (Rookie Read-About Science) by Joanne Barkan
- *Will It Float or Sink?* (Rookie Read-About Science) by Melissa Stewart

Week 4
- *Crystals (The Golden Science Close-up Series)* by Robert A. Bell
- *Rock and Minerals (Eye Wonder)* by DK Publishing

Week 5
- *All the Colors of the Rainbow* (Rookie Read-About Science) by Allan Fowler
- *The Magic School Bus Makes A Rainbow: A Book About Color* by Joanna Cole
- *I Love Colors!* (Hello Reader!, Level 1) by Hans Wilhelm

Week 6
- *Freezing and Melting* (First Step Nonfiction) by Robin Nelson
- *Solids, Liquids, And Gases* (Rookie Read-About Science) by Ginger Garrett

Unit 2: Intro to Physics

Week 1
- *Gravity Is a Mystery* (Let's-Read-and-Find... Science 2) by Franklyn M. Branley and Edward Miller
- *What Is Gravity?* (Rookie Read-About Science) by Lisa Trumbauer
- *Gravity* (Blastoff! Readers: First Science) by Kay Manolis
- *Galileo's Leaning Tower Experiment* (Junior Library Guild Selection) by Wendy Macdonald and Paolo Rui

Week 2
- *Magnets* (All Aboard Science Reader) by Anne Schreiber and Adrian C. Sinnott
- *What Makes a Magnet?* (Let's-Read-and-Find... Science 2) by Franklyn M. Branley and True Kelley
- *Magnets: Pulling Together, Pushing Apart* (Amazing Science) by Natalie M. Boyd

Week 3
- *Inclined Planes to the Rescue* (First Facts) by Thales and Sharon
- *Inclined Planes and Wedges* (Early Bird Physics Series) by Sally M. Walker
- *What are Inclined Planes?* (Looking at Simple Machines) by Helen Frost

Week 4
- *The Magic School Bus and the Electric Field Trip* by Joanna Cole

Week 5
- *Pull, Lift, and Lower: A Book About Pulleys* (Amazing Science: Simple Machines) by Dahl
- *What Is a Pulley?* (Welcome Books) by Lloyd G. Douglas

Week 6
- *All About Light* (Rookie Read-About Science) by Lisa Trumbauer
- *Exploring Light* (How Does Science Work?) by Carol Ballard
- *The Magic School Bus: Gets A Bright Idea, The: A Book About Light* by Nancy White

Unit 3: Intro to Geology

Week 1
- *Mary Anning: Fossil Hunter* by Sally M. Walker and Phyllis V. Saroff
- *Viewfinder: Fossils* by Douglas Palmer and Neil D. L. Clark
- *What Do You Know About Fossils?* (20 Questions: Science) by Suzanne Slade
- *Fossils Tell of Long Ago* (Let's-Read-and-Find Out Science 2) by Aliki

Week 2
- *Looking at Rocks* (My First Field Guides) by Jennifer Dussling and Tim Haggerty
- *Rocks: Hard, Soft, Smooth, and Rough* (Amazing Science) by Rosinsky, Natalie M, John, and Matthew
- *Rocks and Fossils* (Science Kids) by Chris Pellant
- *Rocks! Rocks! Rocks!* by Nancy Elizabeth Wallace

Week 3
- *Metamorphic Rocks* (Earth Rocks!) by Holly Cefrey
- *I Love Rocks* (Rookie Readers, Level B) by Cari Meister and Terry Sirrell

Week 4
- *National Geographic Readers: Volcanoes!* by Anne Schreiber
- *Jump into Science: Volcano!* by Ellen J. Prager and Nancy Woodman
- *Volcanoes* (Let's-Read-and-Find... Science 2) by Franklyn M. Branley and Megan Lloyd
- *The Magic School Bus Blows Its Top: A Book About Volcanoes* (Magic School Bus) by Gail Herman and Bob Ostrom

Week 5
- *Sedimentary Rocks* (Earth Rocks!) by Holly Cefrey
- *Earthsteps: A Rock's Journey through Time* by Diane Nelson Spickert and Marianne D. Wallace

Week 6
- *You Can Use a Compass* (Rookie Read-About Science) by Lisa Trumbauer
- *North, South, East, and West* (Rookie Read-About Science) by Allan Fowler
- *Maps and Globes* by Jack Knowlton and Harriet Barton

Unit 4: Intro to Meteorlogy

Week 1
- *The Sun: Our Nearest Star* (Let's-Read-and-Find Out) by Franklyn M. Branley and Edward Miller
- *Wake Up, Sun!* (Step-Into-Reading, Step 1) by David L. Harrison
- *The Sun Is My Favorite Star* by Frank Asch

Week 2
- *The Water Cycle* (First Facts, Water All Around) by Rebecca Olien
- *The Magic School Bus Wet All Over: A Book About The Water Cycle* by Pat Relf and Carolyn Bracken

Week 3
- *Watching the Seasons* (Welcome Books) by Edana Eckart
- *Sunshine Makes the Seasons* (Let's-Read-and-Find... Science 2) by Franklyn M. Branley and Michael Rex
- *Our Seasons* by Ranida T. Mckneally and Grace Lin

Week 4
- *Feel the Wind* (Let's-Read-and-Find... Science 2) by Arthur Dorros
- *The Wind Blew* by Pat Hutchins
- *Can You See the Wind?* (Rookie Read-About Science) by Allan Fowler

Week 5
- *Tornado Alert* (Let's-Read-and-Find... Science 2) by Franklyn M. Branley and Giulio Maestro
- *Tornados!* (DK READERS) by DK Publishing
- *The Terrifying Tub Tornado* by Ann K. Larson

Week 6
- *What Is a Thermometer* (Rookie Read-About Science) by Lisa Trumbauer
- *Thermometers* (First Facts. Science Tools) by Adele Richardson
- *Temperature* (Blastoff! Readers, First Science) by Kay Manolis
- *Too, Too Hot* (Reader's Clubhouse Level 1 Reader) by Judy Kentor Schmauss

Unit 5: Intro to Botany

Week 1
- *From Seed to Plant* (Rookie Read-About Science) by Allan Fowler
- *From Seed to Plant* by Gail Gibbons

Week 2
- *The Reason for a Flower* (Ruth Heller's World of Nature) by Ruth Heller
- *Planting a Rainbow* by Lois Ehler

Week 3
- *The Magic School Bus Plants Seeds: A Book About How Living Things Grow* by Joanna Cole
- *Seeds* by Ken Robbins
- *A Fruit Is a Suitcase for Seeds* by Jean Richards and Anca Hariton
- *Curious George Plants a Seed* (Curious George Early Readers) by H. A. Rey

Week 4
- *Leaves* (Plant Parts series) (Pebble Plus: Plant Parts) by Vijaya Bodach,
- *I Am A Leaf* (Level 1 - Hello Reader) by Jean Marzollo and Judith Moffatt
- *Leaves* by David Ezra Stein

Week 5
- *Stems* (Plant Parts) by Vijaya Bodach
- *Plant Stems & Roots* (Look Once, Look Again Science Series) by David M. Schwartz
- *Stems* (First Step Nonfiction) by Melanie Mitchell

Week 6
- *Roots* (First Step Nonfiction) by Melanie Mitchell
- *Roots* (Plant Parts series) (Pebble Plus: Plant Parts) by Vijaya Bodach
- *Plant Plumbing: A Book About Roots and Stems* (Growing Things) by Susan Blackaby and Charlene Delage

Unit 6: Intro to Zoology

Week 1
- *What's It Like to Be a Fish?* (Let's-Read-and-Find... Science 1) by Wendy Pfeffer
- *Rainbow Fish Big Book* by Marcus Pfister Herbert and J. Alison James
- *Fish Eyes: A Book You Can Count On* by Lois Ehlert

Week 2
- *Butterfly House* by Eve Bunting and Greg Shed
- *A Butterfly Grows* (Green Light Readers Level 2) by Stephen R. Swinburne
- *From Caterpillar to Butterfly: Following the Life Cycle* by Suzanne Slade
- *The Life of a Butterfly* by Clare Hibbert

Week 3
- *No Backbone! the World of Invertebrates* by Natalie Lunis
- *I Wonder What It's Like to Be an Earthworm* (Hovanec, Erin M. Life Science Wonder Series.) by Erin M. Hovanec
- *Are You a Snail?* (Backyard Books) by Judy Allen

Week 4
- *About Mammals: A Guide For Children* by Cathryn Sill and John Sill
- *Eye Wonder: Mammals* (Eye Wonder) by Sarah Walker
- *Is a Camel a Mammal?* by Tish Rabe and Jim Durk
- *Animals Called Mammals* (What Kind of Animal Is It?) by Bobbie Kalman

Week 5
- *Miles and Miles of Reptiles: All About Reptiles* by Tish Rabe and Aristides Ruiz

- *Eye Wonder: Reptiles* (Eye Wonder) by Simon Holland
- *Reptiles* (True Books : Animals) by Melissa Stewart
- *Fun Facts About Snakes!* (I Like Reptiles and Amphibians!) by Carmen Bredeson

Week 6
- *About Birds: A Guide for Children* by Cathryn Sill and John Sill
- *Fine Feathered Friends: All About Birds* by Tish Rabe
- *How Do Birds Find Their Way?* (Let's-Read-and-Find... Science 2) by Roma Gans
- *The Magic School Bus Flies from the Nest* by Joanna Cole and Carolyn Bracken

Intro to Science
Unit 1: Intro to Chemistry

Intro to Chemistry Unit Overview

Sequence for Study
- Week 1: Solids and liquids
- Week 2: Solutions
- Week 3: Density
- Week 4: Crystals
- Week 5: Colors
- Week 6: Freezing

Supplies Needed for the Unit

Week	Introduction Props	Hands-on Project Materials	Coordinating Activities Supplies
1	Ice, Crayon	Crayons, Muffin tin	Paper, Popsicles, Chocolate or Crackers
2	Plate, Paintbrush, Cup	Powdered drink mix, Measuring spoons, Clear cups, Spoons, Dirt, Water	Pudding mix, Milk, Several cups, Lemonade, Paint (one color and white), Paintbrush, Dirt
3	Glass jar, Water, Spoon, Oil	Glass jar, Water, Oil, Objects to test, Bucket of water	Chalk, Water, Paper, 9 by 13 Pan, Several types of fruit, Glass jar, Oil, Water, Food coloring
4	Pictures of various types of crystals (or several rocks with crystals)	Sponge, Ammonia, Salt, Water, Liquid bluing, Pie pan, Measuring cup and spoon, Quartz	2 Bowls, Sugar, Salt, Paper, Sparkly markers, Glitter
5	3 Glasses, Food coloring (blue and yellow)	Several clear glasses, Dish pan, Food coloring (red, yellow, and blue), Prism	Sugar cookies, Icing in different colors, Shallow dish, Milk, Food coloring (red, yellow, and blue), Liquid dish soap, Paint (red, yellow, and blue), Paper
6	Ice, Plate	Several small film canisters, Various household liquids, Small box lined with foil	Various frozen foods, Food coloring, Water, Paper cup, Popsicle stick, Fruit juice, Paper

Books Scheduled

Hands-on Projects (Required Books)
- *More Mudpies to Magnets (If you are using the scientific demonstration option.)*
- *Handbook of Nature Study (If you are using the nature study option.)*

Read-Aloud Suggestions

Optional Encyclopedia
- *The Usborne Children's Encyclopedia*

Week 1
- *What is the world made of? All about solids, liquids and gases (Let's Read and Find out About Science)* by Kathleen Weidner Zoehfeld and Paul Meisel
- *Change It!: Solids, Liquids, Gases and You (Primary Physical Science)* by Adrienne Mason and Claudia Davila
- *Solids, Liquids and Gases (Starting with Science)* by Ray Boudreau

Week 2
- *Liquids (States of Matter)* by Carol Ryback and Jim Mezzanotte
- *Lulu's Lemonade (Math Matters)* by Barbara Derubertis and Paige Billin-Frye

Week 3
- *What Is Density? (Rookie Read-About Science)* by Joanne Barkan
- *Will It Float or Sink? (Rookie Read-About Science)* by Melissa Stewart

Week 4
- *Crystals (The Golden Science Close-up Series)* by Robert A. Bell
- *Rock and Minerals (Eye Wonder)* by DK Publishing

Week 5
- *All the Colors of the Rainbow (Rookie Read-About Science)* by Allan Fowler
- *The Magic School Bus Makes A Rainbow: A Book About Color* by Joanna Cole
- *I Love Colors! (Hello Reader!, Level 1)* by Hans Wilhelm

Week 6
- *Freezing and Melting (First Step Nonfiction)* by Robin Nelson
- *Solids, Liquids, And Gases (Rookie Read-About Science)* by Ginger Garrett

Solids and Liquids ~ Week 1

Weekly Topic

Main Idea
- A solid melts into a liquid.

Introduction
Have a piece of ice and a crayon on a plate in front of each student. Say to the students:

This week, we are going to look closer at solids and liquids. The ice and the crayon in front of us are both solids. Ice is solid water, where as the crayon is made from solid wax. When ice gets warm, it melts and turns into liquid water. See how that's happening right in front of us? This process is called melting.

Let them play with the ice and see firsthand how it is turning into a liquid. Then, ask the students:

? *Is the crayon in front of us melting?*

Then, say:

That's right! The crayon needs more heat before it will melt and become a liquid. This week, we are going to turn our solid wax crayon into liquid wax by melting it. Then we are going to let it cool and see what happens!

Student Diary Assignment
- Have the students color the coloring page found on SD pg. 6.

Lapbook Assignment
- Have the students cut out and color the Solids and Liquids Mini-book on LT pg. 7. You can have them cut out the main idea graphic included and glue it in the interior of the mini-book or you can write a sentence with what they have learned from the week for them on the inside of the mini-book. Once the students are done, have them glue the booklet into the mini-lapbook.

Hands-on Projects

Scientific Demonstration: Crayon Cookies

In this demonstration, you will help the students to see how solids melt into liquids and then cool to form solids again. (*Note – Keep your crayon cookies for use later in the week.*)

Materials Needed
- ✓ Crayons
- ✓ Muffin tin

Steps to Complete
1. Follow the directions found on *More Mudpies to Magnets* pg. 38.

Student Diary Assignment
- ☐ With the students, fill out the demonstration sheet found on SD pg. 7.

Nature Study: Finding Wax Coatings

This year, your nature study time will mainly focus on developing the students' awareness of the world around them. For your own personal knowledge about guiding nature study, I recommend that you read pp. 1-23 in the Handbook of Nature Study.

Preparation
- Waxy coatings can be found in nature on most pine trees, so that is the focus of your nature study this week. Read pp. 670-674 in the *Handbook of Nature Study* to learn more about pine trees.

Outdoor Time
- Go on a walk with the students to see if you can find any pine trees to observe. Allow the students to observe the tree and ask any questions they may have. You can use the information you have learned from reading the *Handbook of Nature Study* to answer their questions or to share information about what they are observing.

Student Diary Assignment
- ☐ With the students, fill out the nature journal sheet found on SD pg. 9. The students can sketch what they have seen or you can write down their observations.

Read-Alouds

Optional Encyclopedia Pages
- *The Usborne Children's Encyclopedia* pp.188-189 Solids, liquids, and gases

Optional Library Books
- *What is the world made of? All about solids, liquids and gases (Let's Read and Find out About Science)* by Kathleen Weidner Zoehfeld and Paul Meisel
- *Change It!: Solids, Liquids, Gases and You (Primary Physical Science)* by Adrienne Mason and Claudia Davila
- *Solids, Liquids and Gases (Starting with Science)* by Ray Boudreau

Coordinating Activities

These following activities will help you to reinforce the week's topic and main idea.

- **Art** – (Coloring with Cookies) Give the students their crayon cookies they made during their experiment. Let them color a picture of their choice using their crayon cookies.

  Student Diary Assignment
  - Have the students use SD pg. 8 to complete the art activity.

  Lapbook Assignment
  - Have the students cut out the "My Chemistry Projects" pocket on LT pg. 13. Have them glue the pocket into the lapbook and add the coloring project they just did to the pocket.

- **Snack** – (Solid Popsicles) Point out to the students that popsicles are solid, ask what happens when they take a bit of their popsicle and let it sit in their mouth for minute.

- **Game** – (Will it melt?) Let the students choose several foods that they want to see melt (such as chocolate or crackers). Place them in a muffin tin and heat them in the oven for five minutes, watching carefully. Observe what happens.

Notes

Possible Schedules for Week 1

Two Days a Week Schedule	
Day 1	Day 2
❏ Read the introduction with the students. Color the main idea page. ❏ Complete the Hands-on Project "Crayon Cookies" and fill out the demonstration sheet.	❏ Complete the Hands-on Project: Nature Study "Finding Waxy Coatings" and fill out the nature journal sheet. ❏ Do the "Coloring with Cookies" activity.
Supplies Needed for the Week ✓ Day 1: Ice, Crayons, Muffin tin ✓ Day 2: Paper	

Five Days a Week Schedule				
Day 1	Day 2	Day 3	Day 4	Day 5
❏ Read the introduction with the students. Color the main idea page. ❏ Eat "Solid Popsicles" for snack.	❏ Complete the Hands-on Project "Crayon Cookies" and fill out the demonstration sheet. ❏ Read the selected pages in *The Usborne Children's Encyclopedia*.	❏ Play a game of "Will it melt?". ❏ Complete the Solid and Liquids Mini-book. ❏ Choose one of the books from the read-aloud suggestions and read it to the students.	❏ Do the "Coloring with Cookies" activity. ❏ Choose one of the books from the read-aloud suggestions and read it to the students.	❏ Complete the Hands-on Project: Nature Study "Finding Waxy Coatings" and fill out the nature journal sheet.
Supplies Needed for the Week ✓ Day 1: Ice, Crayon, Popsicles ✓ Day 2: Crayons, Muffin tin ✓ Day 3: Chocolate, Sugar, or Crackers ✓ Day 4: Paper				

Solutions ~ Week 2

Weekly Topic

Main Idea

- Adding water to a solution will make it thinner or weaker.

Introduction

Have some thick paint on a plate, paintbrush, and a cup of water in front of each student. Say to the students:

This paint is really thick, isn't it? Why don't you try using this to paint over the gray line on the top of your Student Diary page.

Let the students paint a line on SD pg. 10 with the thick paint on the paper. Then say:

Now, I want to make a thinner paint solution so that it is easier for us to use as we paint. I am going to add a little water from this cup to our paint solution. Let's see what happens!

Add the water and let the students use the paint brush to mix the paint and water. Then ask the students:

? *Did the paint get thinner?*

You are right, the paint did get thinner! The scientific word for this is "diluted." We diluted the paint with water to make it thinner. This week, we are going to look closer at solutions and dilutions. But before we do that, why don't you use our diluted paint solution to paint over the other gray line on the bottom of the Student Diary page.

Student Diary Assignment

- Have the students complete the coloring page found on SD pg. 10.

Lapbook Assignment

- Have the students cut out and color the Solutions Mini-book on LT pg. 8. You can have them cut out the main idea graphic included and glue it in the interior of the mini-book or you can write a sentence with what they have learned from the week for them on the inside of the mini-book. Once the students are done, have them glue the booklet into the mini-lapbook.

Hands-on Projects

Scientific Demonstration: Kool-Aid Chemistry

In this demonstration, you will help the students to see how solutions can be diluted.

Materials Needed
- ✓ Powdered drink mix (preferably pre-sweetened)
- ✓ Measuring spoons
- ✓ Clear cups
- ✓ Water
- ✓ Spoons

Steps to Complete
1. Follow the directions found on *More Mudpies to Magnets* pg. 44.

Student Diary Assignment
- ☐ With the students, fill out the demonstration sheet found on SD pg. 11.

Nature Study: Mud is a solution

This week, you are looking at solutions and mud is a naturally occurring solution! You don't need a mud puddle. Instead, you will examine the dirt, a.k.a. soil, in your backyard and then use that soil to make a solution.

Preparation
- To learn more about soil, read pp. 760-764 in the *Handbook of Nature Study* to learn more about soil.

Outdoor Time
- Go on a walk with the students to collect some soil from your backyard. Observe the soil and then use that soil to make your own mud solutions. You can do this by using different amounts of water to get different thickness of mud. Allow the students to make their own observations about the soil and the mud you made. You can use the information you have learned from reading the *Handbook of Nature Study* to answer their questions or to share information about soil and mud.

Student Diary Assignment
- ☐ With the students, fill out the nature journal sheet found on SD pg. 13. The students can sketch what they have seen or you can write down their observations.

Read-Alouds

Optional Encyclopedia Pages
- *The Usborne Children's Encyclopedia* - There are no new pages scheduled. If you would like, you can re-read the pages (pp. 188-189) on solids, liquids, and gases.

Optional Library Books
- *Liquids* (States of Matter) by Carol Ryback and Jim Mezzanotte
- *Lulu's Lemonade* (Math Matters) by Barbara Derubertis and Paige Billin-Frye

Coordinating Activities

These following activities will help you to reinforce the week's topic and main idea.

- **Art** – (Diluted Art) Give the students a plate with one color of paint and plenty of white paint. Have the students paint first with the original color on a piece of paper. Then, have the students dilute their color with the white paint, making sure to paint with each lighter color as they go along.

    Student Diary Assignment
    - Have the students use SD pg. 12 to complete the art activity.

    Lapbook Assignment
    - Have the students add the page they painted to the "My Chemistry Projects" pocket in the lapbook.

- **Snack** – (Make pudding) Point out to the students that pudding is a solution. Make pudding together by following the directions found on your pudding package. Before you put the mixture in the fridge, remove ¼ cup of the mixture and put it in another bowl. Add an additional ½ cup of milk to that mixture to dilute it, then put both bowls in the fridge. Check the two bowls after two hours and see how they differ.

- **Game** – (Strongest to Weakest) Make your own lemonade in varying strengths. (*You can make the lemonade solutions ahead of time or make it with the students.*) Then, have the students taste and classify them from strongest to weakest.

Notes

Possible Schedules for Week 2

Two Days a Week Schedule	
Day 1	Day 2
❏ Read the introduction with the students. Color the main idea page. ❏ Complete the Hands-on Project "Kool-Aid Chemistry" and fill out the demonstration sheet.	❏ Complete the Hands-on Project: Nature Study "Mud is a Solution" and fill out the nature journal sheet. ❏ Do the "Diluted Art" activity.
Supplies Needed for the Week ✓ Day 1: Paint, Paintbrush, Cup, Powdered drink mix, Measuring spoons, Clear cups, Water, Spoons ✓ Day 2: Paint (one color and white), Paintbrush, Dirt, Water	

Five Days a Week Schedule				
Day 1	Day 2	Day 3	Day 4	Day 5
❏ Read the introduction with the students. Color the main idea page. ❏ Eat "Make pudding" for snack.	❏ Complete the Hands-on Project "Kool-Aid Chemistry" and fill out the demonstration sheet. ❏ Choose one of the books from the read-aloud suggestions and read it to the students.	❏ Play a game of "Strongest to Weakest". ❏ Complete the Solutions Mini-book. ❏ Choose one of the books from the read-aloud suggestions and read it to the students.	❏ Do the "Diluted Art" activity. ❏ Choose one of the books from the read-aloud suggestions and read it to the students.	❏ Complete the Hands-on Project: Nature Study "Mud is a Solution" and fill out the nature journal sheet.
Supplies Needed for the Week ✓ Day 1: Paint, Paintbrush, Cup, Pudding mix, Milk ✓ Day 2: Powdered drink mix, Measuring spoons, Clear cups, Water, Spoons ✓ Day 3: Several cups, Lemonade ✓ Day 4: Paint (one color and white), Paintbrush ✓ Day 5: Dirt, Water				

Density ~ Week 3

Weekly Topic

Main Idea
- Oil is less dense than water.

Introduction
Have a large glass jar with half of a cup of water, a spoon. and half of a cup of oil on a table in front of you. Say to the students:

> *We are going to see if we can float this oil on top of the water here in this jar. Here you hold this spoon over the jar while I pour the oil on it.*

Be sure to pour the oil slowly into the jar to prevent mixing; this way the oil will really float on the water. After you finish pouring about half a cup of oil, ask:

> **?** *What's happening, is the oil sinking to the bottom or floating on top of the water?*

That's right, the oil is floating on top of the water. This is because of density!

Density tells us how much space an object takes up compared to how much stuff in is the object. The stuff in the oil is not as closely packed together compared to the stuff in the water. In chemistry, we say that oil is less dense than water. This week, we are going to take a closer look at density.

(***Note*** *– The demonstration for this week uses a jar of oil and water. You can save this jar of oil and water for that demonstration or just pour it out.*)

Student Diary Assignment
- Have the students color the coloring page found on SD pg. 14.

Lapbook Assignment
- Have the students cut out and color the Density Mini-book on LT pg. 9. You can have them cut out the main idea graphic included and glue it in the interior of the mini-book or you can write a sentence with what they have learned from the week for them on the inside of the mini-book. Once the students are done, have them glue the booklet into the mini-lapbook.

Hands-on Projects

Scientific Demonstration: How Dense is Density

In this demonstration, you will help the students to see how density effects whether an object will sink or float.

Materials Needed
- Glass jar
- Water
- Oil
- Objects to test, such as cork, apple slice, paper clip, grape, piece of candle, small rubber eraser, spoon, pencil, paper

Steps to Complete
1. Follow the directions found on *More Mudpies to Magnets* pg. 45.

Student Diary Assignment
- With the students, fill out the demonstration sheet found on SD pg. 15.

Nature Study: Density in Nature

This week, you are looking at density, and objects found in nature also have density. So, for your nature study this week, you will find objects and test their density.

Preparation
- Make sure that you have access to a bucket of water or a pond for testing.

Outdoor Time
- Go on a walk with the students to collect five different objects, such as a leaf, an acorn, a berry, a stick, and a rock. Observe the objects and arrange them in order from lightest to heaviest. Then, drop each object in a bucket of water or pond to see if it sinks or floats.

Student Diary Assignment
- With the students, fill out the nature journal sheet found on SD pg. 17. The students can sketch the objects on the chart or write the names. Then, have them add a check under the column showing if the object sinks or floats.

Read-Alouds

Optional Encyclopedia Pages
- *The Usborne Children's Encyclopedia* pp. 200-201 (Floating)

Optional Library Books

- *What Is Density?* (Rookie Read-About Science) by Joanne Barkan
- *Will It Float or Sink?* (Rookie Read-About Science) by Melissa Stewart

Coordinating Activities

These following activities will help you to reinforce the week's topic and main idea.

✂ **Art** – (Marbled Paper) Powdered chalk is less dense than water and will float on top of it. Begin by grating several colors of chalk over a 9 by 13 pan filled with water. Then, gently swirl the colors and place a piece of paper on the top of the water. Pull the paper out and set it on some paper towels to dry. (*The chalk will transfer to the paper, making your piece of paper appear to be marbled.*)

Student Diary Assignment
- Once the paper is dry, have the students cut out a piece of it and glue it onto the sheet found on SD pg. 16.

Lapbook Assignment
- Have the students add the marbled page to the "My Chemistry Projects" pocket in the lapbook.

✂ **Snack** – (Density in Food) Have several types of fruit set out, such as an apple, a grape, an orange, a pear, or a banana. Have the students examine each fruit and observe how tightly packed the fruit pieces seem. Guide them through rating which fruit is most dense down to which is the least dense. Eat them in order to see if you're correct!

✂ **More Fun** – (Floating Rainbows) Do another demonstration with the students from *More Mudpies to Magnets* pg. 31 (Floating Rainbows.) This demonstration will look at how food coloring bubbles float through oil and water. You will need a glass jar, oil, water, and food coloring.

Notes

Possible Schedules for Week 3

Two Days a Week Schedule	
Day 1	Day 2
❏ Read the introduction with the students. Color the main idea page. ❏ Complete the Hands-on Project "How Dense is Density" and fill out the demonstration sheet.	❏ Complete the Hands-on Project: Nature Study "Density in Nature" and fill out the nature journal sheet. ❏ Do the "Marbled Paper" activity.
Supplies Needed for the Week ✓ Day 1: Glass jar, Water, Oil, Objects to test ✓ Day 2: Chalk, Water, Paper, 9 by 13 Pan, Bucket of water	

Five Days a Week Schedule				
Day 1	Day 2	Day 3	Day 4	Day 5
❏ Read the introduction with the students. Color the main idea page. ❏ Eat "Density in Food" for snack.	❏ Complete the Hands-on Project "How Dense is Density" and fill out the demonstration sheet. ❏ Read the selected pages in *The Usborne Children's Encyclopedia*.	❏ Have some more fun with the "Floating Rainbows" demonstration. ❏ Complete the Density Mini-book. ❏ Choose one of the books from the read-aloud suggestions and read it to the students.	❏ Do the "Marbled Paper" activity. ❏ Choose one of the books from the read-aloud suggestions and read it to the students.	❏ Complete the Hands-on Project: Nature Study "Density in Nature" and fill out the nature journal sheet.
Supplies Needed for the Week ✓ Day 1: Glass jar, Water, Spoon, Oil, Several types of fruit ✓ Day 2: Glass jar, Water, Oil, Objects to test ✓ Day 3: Glass jar, Oil, Water, Food coloring ✓ Day 4: Chalk, Water, Paper, 9 by 13 Pan ✓ Day 5: Bucket of water				

Crystals ~ Week 4

Weekly Topic

Main Idea
- Crystals are made up of minerals found in the earth.

Introduction

Have pictures of various types of crystals from books and magazines (or have several rocks with crystals) on the table in front of you. Say to the students:

This week, we are going to look closer at crystals. These pictures are of (rocks have) crystals.

? *What do you notice about crystals?*

Give them time to observe the pictures (or rocks) before you say:

Those are some good observations. Crystals are formed from minerals found in the earth. They are found in salt, quartz, mica and so many other types of rocks. This week, we are going to look at and grow our own crystals!

Student Diary Assignment
- Have the students color the coloring page found on SD pg. 18.

Lapbook Assignment
- Have the students cut out and color the Crystal Mini-book on LT pg. 10. You can have them cut out the main idea graphic included and glue it in the interior of the mini-book or you can write a sentence with what they have learned from the week for them on the inside of the mini-book. Once the students are done, have them glue the booklet into the mini-lapbook.

Hands-on Projects

Scientific Demonstration: How fast does your crystal grow

In this demonstration, you will help the students to see how crystals are formed. This experiment will become more noticeable as time goes by and can be observed for up to a week.

Materials Needed
- ✓ Sponge

- ✓ Ammonia
- ✓ Salt
- ✓ Water
- ✓ Liquid bluing (*You can find this down the laundry aisle.*)
- ✓ Pie pan
- ✓ Measuring cup and spoon

Steps to Complete
1. Follow the directions found on *More Mudpies to Magnets* pg. 46.

Student Diary Assignment
- ☐ With the students, fill out the demonstration sheet found on SD pg. 19.

Nature Study: Quartz

This week, you are looking for a natually-occuring crystal: quartz. If quartz is not easy to find in your area, have a piece on hand to observe.

Preparation
- Read pp. 754-755 in the *Handbook of Nature Study* to learn more about quartz.

Outdoor Time
- Go on a walk with the students to see if you can find any quartz. Allow the students to observe the quartz rocks they find and ask any questions they may have. You can use the information you have learned from reading the *Handbook of Nature Study* to answer their questions or to share information about what they are observing.

Student Diary Assignment
- ☐ With the students, fill out the nature journal sheet found on SD pg. 21. The students can sketch what they have seen or you can write down their observations.

Read-Alouds

Optional Encyclopedia Pages
- *The Usborne Children's Encyclopedia* - There are no new pages scheduled.

Optional Library Books
- *Crystals (The Golden Science Close-up Series)* by Robert A. Bell
- *Rock and Minerals (Eye Wonder)* by DK Publishing

Coordinating Activities

These following activities will help you to reinforce the week's topic and main idea.

- ✂ Art – (Sparkling Rocks) Have the students draw their own "rocks" on a piece of paper. Then, let them add crystals to their rocks by using sparkly markers and glitter.

  Student Diary Assignment
  - ☐ Have the students use SD pg. 20 to complete this activity.

  Lapbook Assignment
  - 📂 Have the students add the page with their sparkling rocks to the "My Chemistry Projects" pocket in the lapbook.

- ✂ Snack – (Edible Crystals) Set out two small bowls of sugar and salt. Let the students use their five senses to observe more about the two. Allow them to use a magnifying glass to look closer at the crystals. Explain to the students that these are two crystals that we can eat. (*Be sure to remind the studentss that not all crystals are safe to eat and they should always ask you before trying to eat any kind of crystals.*)

- ✂ Game – (Crystal Hunt) Take a walk around your house and see what crystals you can find. You can look for things like crystals in jewelry, rock collections, pictures, magazines, and even in the kitchen.

Notes

Possible Schedules for Week 4

Two Days a Week Schedule	
Day 1	Day 2
❑ Read the introduction with the students. Color the main idea page. ❑ Complete the "How Fast Does Your Crystal Grow" and fill out the demonstration sheet.	❑ Complete the Hands-on Project: Nature Study "Quartz" and fill out the nature journal sheet. ❑ Do the "Sparkling Rocks" activity.
Supplies Needed for the Week ✓ Day 1: Pictures of various types of crystals (or several rocks with crystals), Sponge, Ammonia, Salt, Water, Liquid bluing, Pie pan, Measuring cup and spoon ✓ Day 2: Paper, Sparkly markers, Glitter, Piece of quartz	

Five Days a Week Schedule				
Day 1	Day 2	Day 3	Day 4	Day 5
❑ Read the introduction with the students. Color the main idea page. ❑ Eat "Edible Crystals" for snack.	❑ Complete the Hands-on Project "How Fast Does Your Crystal Grow" and fill out the demonstration sheet. ❑ Choose one of the books from the read-aloud suggestions and read it to the students.	❑ Play a game of "Crystal Hunt". ❑ Complete the Crystals Mini-book. ❑ Choose one of the books from the read-aloud suggestions and read it to the students.	❑ Do the "Sparkling Rocks" activity. ❑ Choose one of the books from the read-aloud suggestions and read it to the students.	❑ Complete the Hands-on Project: Nature Study "Quartz" and fill out the nature journal sheet.
Supplies Needed for the Week ✓ Day 1: Pictures of various types of crystals (or several rocks with crystals) ✓ Day 2: Sponge, Ammonia, Salt, Water, Liquid bluing, Pie pan, Measuring cup, Spoon ✓ Day 3: 2 Bowls, Sugar, Salt ✓ Day 4: Paper, Sparkly markers, Glitter ✓ Day 5: Piece of quartz				

Colors ~ Week 5

Weekly Topic

Main Idea
- Two colors can be mixed to make a new color.

Introduction
Have 3 clear glasses, one half filled with yellow water, one half filled with blue water and one empty on the table in front of you. Say to the students:

In front of me are two glasses with different colored water and one empty glass. Both yellow and blue are primary colors. Let's be color chemists and see what happens when we pour the two colors into the empty glass.

You can pour both or let the students do the pouring. Either way, when you are done ask the students:

? *What color did we make?*

That's right, green is a secondary color because it is made by mixing two primary colors. We mixed yellow and blue to make a new color, green. This week, we are going look at what happens when we mix colors.

You may want to also introduce the color wheel and rainbows at this time.

Student Diary Assignment
- Have the students color the beakers with the colors they observed on the coloring page found on SD pg. 22.

Lapbook Assignment
- Have the students cut out and color the Colors Mini-book on LT pg. 11. You can have them cut out the main idea graphic included and glue it in the interior of the mini-book or you can write a sentence with what they have learned from the week for them on the inside of the mini-book. Once the students are done, have them glue the booklet into the mini-lapbook.

Hands-on Projects

Scientific Demonstration: Colored Water Chemistry

In this demonstration, you will help the students to see what happens when you mix different colors.

Materials Needed
- ✓ Several clear glasses
- ✓ Dish pan
- ✓ Food coloring (red, yellow, and blue)

Steps to Complete
1. Follow the directions found on *More Mudpies to Magnets* pg. 47.

Student Diary Assignment
- ☐ With the students, fill out the demonstration sheet found on SD pg. 23.

Nature Study: Colors in Nature

This week, you are looking at colors and how they mix to form new colors. Rainbows are good examples of primary and secondary colors in nature, so this week your nature study time will focus on that.

Preparation
- ✎ Have a prism on hand in case you don't find a rainbow.

Outdoor Time
- ☼ Go on a walk with the students to see if you can find a rainbow. If you're lucky enough to see one in the sky, allow them to make their own observations and then sketch the rainbow in their nature journal. If not, look at the edges of the clouds for rainbows or find a sunny spot and use a prism to create a rainbow on a sidewalk.

Student Diary Assignment
- ☐ With the students, fill out the nature journal sheet found on SD pg. 25. The students can sketch what they have seen or you can write down their observations.

Read-Alouds

Optional Encyclopedia Pages
- 📖 *The Usborne Children's Encyclopedia* pp. 206-207 (Light and Color)

Optional Library Books
- 📖 *All the Colors of the Rainbow* (Rookie Read-About Science) by Allan Fowler
- 📖 *The Magic School Bus Makes A Rainbow: A Book About Color* by Joanna Cole
- 📖 *I Love Colors!* (Hello Reader!, Level 1) by Hans Wilhelm

Coordinating Activities

These following activities will help you to reinforce the week's topic and main idea.

✂ Art – (Color Painting) Give each student a paper plate with a little red, yellow and blue paint on it. Have them mix the colors to make orange, green and purple. Then, let them paint their own rainbow.

Student Diary Assignment
- Have the students use SD pg. 24 to complete this activity.

Lapbook Assignment
- Have the students add the page they painted to the "My Chemistry Projects" pocket in the lapbook.

✂ Snack – (Color Cookies) Make sugar cookies using your favorite recipe or purchase them from the store. Give the students several bowls with a little bit of white icing in each. Let them choose which colors to add to their icing. Then decorate the cookies with the different colors they created.

✂ More Fun – (Making Rainbows) Pour milk in a bowl. Place three drops of red, yellow and blue food coloring in 3 different places in the bowl. Add a drop of liquid dish soap and watch the colors mix.

Notes

Possible Schedules for Week 5

Two Days a Week Schedule	
Day 1	Day 2
❏ Read the introduction with the students. Color the main idea page. ❏ Complete the Hands-on Project "Colored Water Chemistry" and fill out the demonstration sheet.	❏ Complete the Hands-on Project: Nature Study "Colors in Nature" and fill out the nature journal sheet. ❏ Do the "Color Painting" activity.
Supplies Needed for the Week ✓ Day 1: 3 glasses, Dish pan, Food coloring (red, yellow, and blue) ✓ Day 2: Paint (red, yellow, and blue), Paper, Prism	

Five Days a Week Schedule				
Day 1	Day 2	Day 3	Day 4	Day 5
❏ Read the introduction with the students. Color the main idea page. ❏ Eat "Color Cookies" for snack.	❏ Complete the Hands-on Project "Colored Water Chemistry" and fill out the demonstration sheet. ❏ Read the selected pages in *The Usborne Children's Encyclopedia*.	❏ Have some more fun with the "Making Rainbows" demonstration. ❏ Complete the Colors Mini-book. ❏ Choose one of the books from the read-aloud suggestions and read it to the students.	❏ Do the "Color Painting" activity. ❏ Choose one of the books from the read-aloud suggestions and read it to the students.	❏ Complete the Hands-on Project: Nature Study "Colors in Nature" and fill out the nature journal sheet.
Supplies Needed for the Week ✓ Day 1: 3 glasses, Food coloring (blue and yellow), Sugar cookies, Icing in different colors ✓ Day 2: Several clear glasses, Dish pan, Food coloring (red, yellow, and blue) ✓ Day 3: Shallow dish, Milk, Food coloring (red, yellow, and blue), Liquid dish soap ✓ Day 4: Paint (red, yellow, and blue), Paper ✓ Day 5: Prism				

Freezing ~ Week 6

Weekly Topic

Main Idea
- When water freezes, it changes into ice.

Introduction
Have a few cubes of ice on a plate on the table in front of you. Say to the students:

Did you know that ice is really water? When water freezes, it changes into ice. Today, we are going to make some observations about ice.

Ask the students the following questions as they observe the piece of ice:

- *How does the ice feel?*
- *How does the ice smell?*
- *What color is the piece of ice?*

Let the students touch and observe the ice before saying:

When water freezes, it changes into ice, but as you can see when ice melts it turns back into water! This week, we are going to learn about freezing.

Student Diary Assignment
- Have the students color the coloring page found on SD pg. 26.

Lapbook Assignment
- Have the students cut out and color the Freezing Mini-book on LT pg. 12. You can have them cut out the main idea graphic included and glue it in the interior of the mini-book or you can write a sentence with what they have learned from the week for them on the inside of the mini-book. Once the students are done, have them glue the booklet into the mini-lapbook.

Hands-on Projects

Scientific Demonstration: Brrr-It's Cold

In this demonstration, you will help the students to see what happens to different liquids when they are frozen. (*Note – This demonstration will take several hours to complete.*)

Materials Needed
- ✓ Several small film canisters
- ✓ Various household liquids (i.e., water, milk, liquid soap, oil, ketchup, honey, or mustard)
- ✓ Small box lined with foil

Steps to Complete
1. Follow the directions found on *More Mudpies to Magnets* pg. 48.

Student Diary Assignment
- With the students, fill out the demonstration sheet found on SD pg. 27.

Nature Study: Weather Observation

This week, you will be observing the weather.

Preparation
- Read pp. 808-814 in the *Handbook of Nature Study* to learn more about water's various forms and how it relates to weather.

Outdoor Time
- Go on a walk and observe the weather. Allow the students to make more observations about the weather they see. If they need some help, ask them are there clouds in the sky? If so, what color are they? What is the temperature like today? Talk to the students about how water (rain) falls from the sky. Also explain that when the temperature is cold enough, frozen water falls from the sky and we call that snow.

Student Diary Assignment
- With the students, fill out the nature journal sheet found on SD pg. 29. The students can sketch what they have seen or you can write down their observations.

Read-Alouds

Optional Encyclopedia Pages
- *The Usborne Children's Encyclopedia* pp. 190-191 (How materials change)

Optional Library Books
- *Freezing and Melting* (First Step Nonfiction) by Robin Nelson
- *Solids, Liquids, And Gases* (Rookie Read-About Science) by Ginger Garrett

Coordinating Activities

These following activities will help you to reinforce the week's topic and main idea.

✂ **Art** – (Ice Painting) Ahead of time, use food coloring to make several different colors of water and then freeze the colored water into cubes. Once they are frozen, let the students paint with the ice.

Student Diary Assignment
  ☐ Have the students use SD pg. 28 to complete this activity.

Lapbook Assignment
  📁 Have the students add the page they painted to the "My Chemistry Projects" pocket in the lapbook.

✂ **Snack** – (Frozen Foods) Ahead of time, freeze some of the students' favorite fruits or vegetables (i.e., peas, corn, carrots, grapes, strawberries, or bananas, you could also freeze their favorite cookies or crackers). Serve the frozen food for snack. Have the students taste each one and talk about how it tastes the same and how it tastes different.

✂ **More Fun** – (Crystal Pops) Do another demonstration with the students from *More Mudpies to Magnets* pg. 29 (Crystal Pops.) This demonstration will look at how juice freezes and how popsicles are made. You will need a paper cup, popsicle stick, and fruit juice.

Notes

Possible Schedules for Week 6

Two Days a Week Schedule

Day 1	Day 2
❑ Read the introduction with the students. Color the main idea page. ❑ Complete the Hands-on Project "Brrr-It's Cold" and fill out the demonstration sheet. ❑ Prepare the colored ice cubes for the activity.	❑ Complete the Hands-on Project: Nature Study "Weather Observation" and fill out the nature journal sheet. ❑ Do the "Ice Painting" activity.

Supplies Needed for the Week
- ✓ Day 1: Ice, Plate, Several small film canisters, Various household liquids (i.e., water, milk, liquid soap, oil, ketchup, honey, or mustard), Small box lined with foil, Food coloring
- ✓ Day 2:

Five Days a Week Schedule

Day 1	Day 2	Day 3	Day 4	Day 5
❑ Read the introduction with the students. Color the main idea page. ❑ Eat "Frozen Foods" for snack.	❑ Complete the Hands-on Project "Brrr-It's Cold" and fill out the demonstration sheet. ❑ Read the selected pages in *The Usborne Children's Encyclopedia*.	❑ Have some more fun with the "Crystal Pops" demonstration. ❑ Complete the Freezing Mini-book. ❑ Prepare the colored ice cubes for the activity.	❑ Do the "Ice Painting" activity. ❑ Choose one of the books from the read-aloud suggestions and read it to the students.	❑ Complete the Hands-on Project: Nature Study "Weather Observation" and fill out the nature journal sheet.

Supplies Needed for the Week
- ✓ Day 1: Ice, Plate, Various frozen foods
- ✓ Day 2: Several small film canisters, Various household liquids (i.e., water, milk, liquid soap, oil, ketchup, honey, or mustard), Small box lined with foil
- ✓ Day 3: Food coloring, Water, Paper cup, Popsicle stick, Fruit juice
- ✓ Day 4: Paper

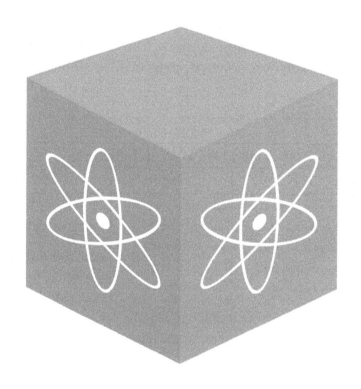

Intro to Science
Unit 2: Intro to Physics

Intro to Physics Unit Overview

Sequence for Study

- Week 1: Gravity
- Week 2: Magnets
- Week 3: Inclined Planes
- Week 4: Static Electricity
- Week 5: Pulleys
- Week 6: Light

Supplies Needed for the Unit

Week	Introduction Props	Hands-on Project Materials	Coordinating Activities Supplies
1	Pencil	Large, soft ball, Marble, Cookie sheet, Chair	Apple, Balloons, Paper, Eyedropper, Paint
2	Bar magnet, Several metal paper clips	String, Magnet, Variety of metal and non-metal objects	Sugar cookie, Red and blue M&M's, Paper, Thin cardboard, Paint, Several magnetic objects, Magnet
3	Long wooden block, Toy car	Different sized balls, Thin board and blocks, Tape or chalk	Graham crackers, Marshmallows, Cookie sheet, Small bowls, Colored water, Eye droppers, Wax paper, Marbles, Plate, Paint, Block, Paper, Thin cardboard
4	Balloon, Cotton shirt	Cork, String, Pin, Metallic paint, Glue, Static electricity producing objects	Wintergreen Lifesaver, Balloon, Cotton shirt, Paper, Glue, Paint brush, Silver glitter
5	Pictures of pulleys	2 Spools of thread, 2 Coat hangers, String, Small basket	Oreo cookies, Licorice rope, Black and brown construction paper, String, Glue
6	(No supplies needed.)	Flat mirror, Flashlight, Tennis ball	Flashlights, Reflective materials, Paper, Glue

Books Scheduled

Hands-on Projects (Required Books)
- *More Mudpies to Magnets* (If you are using the scientific demonstration option.)
- *Handbook of Nature Study* (If you are using the nature study option.)

Read-Aloud Suggestions

Optional Encyclopedia
- *The Usborne Children's Encyclopedia*

Week 1
- *Gravity Is a Mystery* (Let's-Read-and-Find... Science 2) by Franklyn M. Branley and Edward Miller
- *What Is Gravity?* (Rookie Read-About Science) by Lisa Trumbauer
- *Gravity* (Blastoff! Readers: First Science) by Kay Manolis
- *Galileo's Leaning Tower Experiment* (Junior Library Guild Selection) by Wendy Macdonald and Paolo Rui

Week 2
- *Magnets* (All Aboard Science Reader) by Anne Schreiber and Adrian C. Sinnott
- *What Makes a Magnet?* (Let's-Read-and-Find... Science 2) by Franklyn M. Branley and True Kelley
- *Magnets: Pulling Together, Pushing Apart* (Amazing Science) by Natalie M. Boyd

Week 3
- *Inclined Planes to the Rescue* (First Facts) by Thales and Sharon
- *Inclined Planes and Wedges* (Early Bird Physics Series) by Sally M. Walker
- *What are Inclined Planes?* (Looking at Simple Machines) by Helen Frost

Week 4
- *The Magic School Bus and the Electric Field Trip* by Joanna Cole

Week 5
- *Pull, Lift, and Lower: A Book About Pulleys* (Amazing Science: Simple Machines) by Dahl
- *What Is a Pulley?* (Welcome Books) by Lloyd G. Douglas

Week 6
- *All About Light* (Rookie Read-About Science) by Lisa Trumbauer
- *Exploring Light* (How Does Science Work?) by Carol Ballard
- *The Magic School Bus: Gets A Bright Idea, The: A Book About Light* by Nancy White

Gravity ~ Week 1

Weekly Topic

Main Idea
- Gravity is the force that pulls all things to the ground.

Introduction
Have a pencil on the table in front of the student. Say to the student:

Watch what happens when I drop this pencil.

Pick up the pencil, hold it at shoulder height, and let go. Then, ask the student:

? *What happened to the pencil?*

That's right! It fell to the ground. This happened because of gravity.

Gravity is the invisible force that pulls all things to the ground. We can't see it, but it affects us every day. If there was no gravity, we would just float up in the air!

This week, we are going to spend some time learning about gravity.

Student Diary Assignment
- Have the students color the coloring page found on SD pg. 32.

Lapbook Assignment
- Have the students cut out and color the Gravity Mini-book on LT pg. 17. You can have them cut out the main idea graphic included and glue it in the interior of the mini-book or you can write a sentence with what they have learned from the week for them on the inside of the mini-book. Once the students are done, have them glue the booklet into the mini-lapbook.

Hands-on Projects

Scientific Demonstration: Galileo's Drop
In this demonstration, you will help the students to see gravity in action.

Materials Needed
- ✓ Large, soft ball
- ✓ Marble

- ✓ Cookie sheet
- ✓ Chair or stool that is safe to stand on

Steps to Complete
1. Follow the directions found on *More Mudpies to Magnets* pg. 62.

Student Diary Assignment
- With the students, fill out the demonstration sheet found on SD pg. 33.

Nature Study: Apple Tree

This week, you are looking at gravity. Isaac Newton discovered gravity when an apple fell on his head. In honor of his discovery, you are going to study the apple tree this week.

Preparation
- Read the pp. 661-664 in the *Handbook of Nature Study* to learn more about apple trees.

Outdoor Time
- Go on a walk with the students to see if you can find an apple trees to observe. Allow the students to observe the tree and ask any questions they may have. You can use the information you have learned from reading the *Handbook of Nature Study* to answer their questions or to share information about what they are observing.

Student Diary Assignment
- With the students, fill out the nature journal sheet found on SD pg. 35. The students can sketch what they have seen or you can write down their observations.

Read-Alouds

Optional Encyclopedia Pages
- *The Usborne Children's Encyclopedia* pp. 198-199 (Gravity)

Optional Library Books
- *Gravity Is a Mystery* (Let's-Read-and-Find... Science 2) by Franklyn M. Branley and Edward Miller
- *What Is Gravity?* (Rookie Read-About Science) by Lisa Trumbauer
- *Gravity* (Blastoff! Readers: First Science) by Kay Manolis
- *Galileo's Leaning Tower Experiment* (Junior Library Guild Selection) by Wendy Macdonald and Paolo Rui

Coordinating Activities

These following activities will help you to reinforce the week's topic and main idea.

✂ **Art** – (Gravity Drops) Have the students use gravity to paint a picture. Give them an eye dropper and a paint bottle. Using the eye dropper, have the student draw up some paint and then drop the paint on a piece of paper. The student can do this from various heights, but the higher they drop from, the more the paint will splash!

Student Diary Assignment
  Have the students use SD pg. 34 to complete this activity.

Lapbook Assignment
  Have the students cut out the "My Physics Projects" pocket on LT pg. 23. Have them glue the pocket into the lapbook and add the coloring project they just did to the pocket.

✂ **Snack** – (Gravity Apples) Isaac Newton discovered gravity when an apple fell on his head. In honor of his discovery, have apple slices for snack.

✂ **Game** – (Who Can Beat Gravity) You can find directions for this game in *More Mudpies to Magnets* on pg. 63.

Notes

Possible Schedules for Week 1

Two Days a Week Schedule	
Day 1	Day 2
❑ Read the introduction with the students. Color the main idea page. ❑ Complete the Hands-on Project "Galileo's Drop" and fill out the demonstration sheet.	❑ Complete the Hands-on Project: Nature Study "Apple Tree" and fill out the nature journal sheet. ❑ Do the "Gravity Drops" activity.
Supplies Needed for the Week ✓ Day 1: Pencil, Large, soft ball, Marble, Cookie sheet, Chair ✓ Day 2: Eyedropper, Paint, Paper	

Five Days a Week Schedule				
Day 1	Day 2	Day 3	Day 4	Day 5
❑ Read the introduction with the students. Color the main idea page. ❑ Eat "Gravity Apples" for snack.	❑ Complete the Hands-on Project "Galileo's Drop" and fill out the demonstration sheet. ❑ Read the selected pages in *The Usborne Children's Encyclopedia*.	❑ Play a game of "Who can beat gravity?" ❑ Complete the Gravity Mini-book. ❑ Choose one of the books from the read-aloud suggestions and read it to the students.	❑ Do the "Gravity Drops" activity. ❑ Choose one of the books from the read-aloud suggestions and read it to the students.	❑ Complete the Hands-on Project: Nature Study "Apple Tree" and fill out the nature journal sheet.
Supplies Needed for the Week ✓ Day 1: Pencil, Apple ✓ Day 2: Large, soft ball, Marble, Cookie sheet, Chair ✓ Day 3: Balloons, Paper ✓ Day 4: Eyedropper, Paint, Paper				

Intro to Science Unit 2 Intro to Physics ~ Week 1 Gravity

Magnets ~ Week 2

Weekly Topic

Main Idea
- Magnets are attracted to certain kinds of metal.

Introduction

Have a bar magnet and several metal paper clips on the table in front of you. Say to the student:

This is a magnet, which can attract metal! Let's see what happens when we put the magnet near these paper clips.

Hover the magnet over the paper clips until one "jumps" up. Then, ask:

? *What happened?*

That's right! The paper clip jumped up because it was attracted to the magnet.

Magnets are attracted to certain kinds of metal. Paper clips are magnetic, which means that they are attracted to magnets.

Let's see how many paper clips this magnet will hold.

Hold up the magnet and let the students add paper clips until the magnet can't hold any more. When they are done, say:

This week, we are going to spend some time learning about magnets.

Student Diary Assignment
- Have the students color the coloring page found on SD pg. 36.

Lapbook Assignment
- Have the students cut out and color the Magnet Mini-book on LT pg. 18. You can have them cut out the main idea graphic included and glue it in the interior of the mini-book or you can write a sentence with what they have learned from the week for them on the inside of the mini-book. Once the students are done, have them glue the booklet into the mini-lapbook.

Hands-on Projects

Scientific Demonstration: Are you attracted to me?

In this demonstration, you will help the students to see what objects are attracted to a magnet.

Materials Needed
- ✓ String
- ✓ Magnet (bar or horseshoe)
- ✓ Variety of metal and non-metal objects (such as pins, soda cans, coins, cotton, wood, paper, or another magnet)

Steps to Complete
1. Follow the directions found on *More Mudpies to Magnets* pg. 65.

Student Diary Assignment
- ☐ With the students, fill out the demonstration sheet found on SD pg. 37.

Nature Study: Magnetism in Nature

This week, you are looking for objects in nature that are magnetic.

Preparation
- Read the pp. 776-779 in the *Handbook of Nature Study* to learn more about magnets.

Outdoor Time
- Go on a walk with the students to collect various objects to test for magnetism. Allow the students to make the choice of what they want to bring home to test or let them test the materials in the field!

Student Diary Assignment
- ☐ With the students, fill out the nature journal sheet found on SD pg. 39. The students can sketch what they have seen or you can write down their observations.

Read-Alouds

Optional Encyclopedia Pages
- *The Usborne Children's Encyclopedia* pp. 204-205 (Magnets)

Optional Library Books

- *Magnets* (All Aboard Science Reader) by Anne Schreiber and Adrian C. Sinnott
- *What Makes a Magnet?* (Let's-Read-and-Find... Science 2) by Franklyn M. Branley and True Kelley
- *Magnets: Pulling Together, Pushing Apart* (Amazing Science) by Natalie M. Boyd

Coordinating Activities

These following activities will help you to reinforce the week's topic and main idea.

- **Art** – (Painting with Magnets) Collect several magnetic objects, such as a metal washer, a metal ball, and a paper clip, for the student to paint with. Use a piece of paper taped onto a thin sheet of cardboard to give the paper some strength. Have the students dip the metal objects in paint and then put it on the paper. Use a magnet from the underside of the paper to drag the object across the paper so that it "paints" on the paper.

  Student Diary Assignment
  - Have the students use SD pg. 38 to complete this activity.

  Lapbook Assignment
  - Have the students add the page they painted to the "My Physics Projects" pocket in the lapbook.

- **Snack** – (Magnet Cookies) Make your favorite sugar cookie recipe. Use red and blue M&M's to make the design of a magnet on the cookies. Bake and enjoy.
- **Game** – (Magnetic Household) Give the students a magnet and let them walk around your house testing various objects to see if they are magnetic. (*Note – Be sure not to let them use the magnets near computers or other electronics.*)

Notes

Possible Schedules for Week 2

Two Days a Week Schedule

Day 1	Day 2
❏ Read the introduction with the students. Color the main idea page. ❏ Complete the Hands-on Project "Are you attracted to me?" and fill out the demonstration sheet.	❏ Complete the Hands-on Project: Nature Study "Magnetism in Nature" and fill out the nature journal sheet. ❏ Do the "Painting with Magnets" activity.

Supplies Needed for the Week
- ✓ Day 1: Bar magnet, Several metal paper clips, String, Magnet (bar or horseshoe), Variety of metal and non-metal objects
- ✓ Day 2: Paper, Thin cardboard, Paint, Several magnetic objects, Magnet

Five Days a Week Schedule

Day 1	Day 2	Day 3	Day 4	Day 5
❏ Read the introduction with the students. Color the main idea page. ❏ Eat "Magnet Cookies" for snack.	❏ Complete the Hands-on Project "Are you attracted to me?" and fill out the demonstration sheet. ❏ Read the selected pages in *The Usborne Children's Encyclopedia*.	❏ Play a game of "Magnetic Household." ❏ Complete the Magnet Mini-book. ❏ Choose one of the books from the read-aloud suggestions and read it to the students.	❏ Do the "Painting with Magnets" activity. ❏ Choose one of the books from the read-aloud suggestions and read it to the students.	❏ Complete the Hands-on Project: Nature Study "Magnetism in Nature" and fill out the nature journal sheet.

Supplies Needed for the Week
- ✓ Day 1: Bar magnet, Several metal paper clips, Sugar cookie, Red and blue M&M's
- ✓ Day 2: String, Magnet (bar or horseshoe), Variety of metal and non-metal objects
- ✓ Day 3: Magnet
- ✓ Day 4: Paper, Thin cardboard, Paint, Several magnetic objects, Magnet
- ✓ Day 5: Magnet

Inclined Planes ~ Week 3

Weekly Topic

Main Idea
- A ramp is called an inclined plane.

Introduction
Have a long wooden block set up as an inclined plane on the table in front of you. Also have a small toy car to use. Say to the student:

When this car is sitting on the flat surface of the table, it doesn't move. Let's see what happens when I put it at the top of this ramp.

Place the car at the top of the wooden block and let go. Ask the student:

? *What happened?*

You're right! It rolled down the ramp. We call this ramp an inclined plane, which is a type of simple machine. Inclined planes make it easier for us to take an object up or down by spreading out the height over a distance.

This week, we are going to spend some time learning about inclined planes.

Student Diary Assignment
- Have the students color the coloring page found on SD pg. 40.

Lapbook Assignment
- Have the students cut out and color the Inclined Planes Mini-book on LT pg. 19. You can have them cut out the main idea graphic included and glue it in the interior of the mini-book or you can write a sentence with what they have learned from the week for them on the inside of the mini-book. Once the students are done, have them glue the booklet into the mini-lapbook.

Hands-on Projects

Scientific Demonstration: Rolling Along
In this demonstration, you will help the students to learn about inclined planes.

Materials Needed
- ✓ Different sized balls

- ✓ Ramp made from a thin board and blocks
- ✓ Tape or chalk

Steps to Complete
1. Follow the directions found on *More Mudpies to Magnets* pg. 66.

Student Diary Assignment
- ☐ With the students, fill out the demonstration sheet found on SD pg. 41.

Nature Study: Ramps in Nature

This week, you are looking for objects in natural ramps, or inclined planes. These could be found in rock formations, ant hills, drainage ditches, or the edges of a creek.

Preparation
- No preparation this week.

Outdoor Time
- Go on a walk with the students to look for inclined planes in nature. Take some time to roll a small rock or acorn down the inclined planes you find. Allow the students to make observations and discoveries about the inclined planes.

Student Diary Assignment
- ☐ With the students, fill out the nature journal sheet found on SD pg. 43. The students can sketch what they have seen or you can write down their observations.

Read-Alouds

Optional Encyclopedia Pages
- *The Usborne Children's Encyclopedia* - There are no new pages scheduled.

Optional Library Books
- *Inclined Planes to the Rescue* (First Facts) by Thales and Sharon
- *Inclined Planes and Wedges* (Early Bird Physics Series) by Sally M. Walker
- *What are Inclined Planes?* (Looking at Simple Machines) by Helen Frost

Coordinating Activities

These following activities will help you to reinforce the week's topic and main idea.

- Art – (Ramp Painting) Give the student several marbles, a plate with some paint on it, a block of wood and a piece of paper taped onto a thin sheet of cardboard to give it some strength. Have the student set up an inclined plane of paper using the block of wood. Next, roll the marbles in the paint and then roll the marbles down the inclined plane. You could have the student vary the height of the ramp to change the speed of the marble, which will change the type of paint track it leaves behind.

Student Diary Assignment
- Have the students use SD pg. 42 to complete this activity.

Lapbook Assignment
- Have the students add the page they painted to the "My Physics Projects" pocket in the lapbook.

- **Snack** – (Marshmallow Ramps) Give the students several whole graham crackers and a few marshmallows. Have them make an inclined plane out of the graham crackers and test it with their marshmallows. When they are done experimenting, let them eat their creations.
- **Game** – (Water Drop Race) Do another activity from *More Mudpies to Magnets* pg. 71, "Water Drop Race" This experiment will help the students to learn about how water behaves on an inclined plane. You will need a cookie sheet, small bowls, colored water, eye droppers, and wax paper.

Notes

Possible Schedules for Week 3

Two Days a Week Schedule	
Day 1	Day 2
❑ Read the introduction with the students. Color the main idea page. ❑ Complete the Hands-on Project "Rolling Along" and fill out the demonstration sheet.	❑ Complete the Hands-on Project: Nature Study "Ramps in Nature" and fill out the nature journal sheet. ❑ Do the "Ramp Painting" activity.
Supplies Needed for the Week ✓ Day 1: Long wooden block, Toy car, Different sized balls, Thin board and blocks, Tape or chalk ✓ Day 2: Marbles, Plate, Paint, Block, Paper, Thin cardboard	

Five Days a Week Schedule				
Day 1	Day 2	Day 3	Day 4	Day 5
❑ Read the introduction with the students. Color the main idea page. ❑ Eat "Marshmallow Ramps" for snack.	❑ Complete the Hands-on Project "Rolling Along" and fill out the demonstration sheet. ❑ Choose one of the books from the read-aloud suggestions and read it to the students.	❑ Play a game of "Water Drop Race." ❑ Complete the Inclined Planes Mini-book.	❑ Do the "Ramp Painting" activity. ❑ Choose one of the books from the read-aloud suggestions and read it to the students.	❑ Complete the Hands-on Project: Nature Study "Ramps in Nature" and fill out the nature journal sheet.
Supplies Needed for the Week ✓ Day 1: Long wooden block, Toy car, Graham crackers, Marshmallows ✓ Day 2: Different sized balls, Thin board and blocks, Tape or chalk ✓ Day 3: Cookie sheet, Small bowls, Colored water, Eye droppers, Wax paper ✓ Day 4: Marbles, Plate, Paint, Block, Paper, Thin cardboard				

Static Electricity ~ Week 4

Weekly Topic

Main Idea
- Static electricity is an electrical charge that attracts.

Introduction
Have a balloon and a cotton shirt ready to use. Say to the student:

Let's see if we can make this balloon stick to your shirt without any tape or glue!

Rub the balloon vigorously across the shirt for about thirty seconds. Afterward, it should stick to the shirt. If it does, ask the student:

? *What do you think is holding the balloon to the shirt?*

This is a tough question and you will probably get some interesting answers. Let the students come up with an idea or two and then say:

Wow, that is interesting. It isn't magic that holds the balloon in place: it's actually something called static electricity. Static electricity is an electrical charge that attracts. I created this when I rubbed the balloon on your shirt.

This week, we are going to spend some time looking at static electricity.

Student Diary Assignment
- Have the students color the coloring page found on SD pg. 44.

Lapbook Assignment
- Have the students cut out and color the Static Electricity Mini-book on LT pg. 20. You can have them cut out the main idea graphic included and glue it in the interior of the mini-book or you can write a sentence with what they have learned from the week for them on the inside of the mini-book. Once the students are done, have them glue the booklet into the mini-lapbook.

Hands-on Projects

Scientific Demonstration: Static Electricity Tester
In this demonstration, you will help the students to see static electricity.

Materials Needed
- ✓ Cork
- ✓ String
- ✓ Pin
- ✓ Metallic paint
- ✓ Glue
- ✓ Static electricity producing objects, such as wool, rabbit fur, plastic wrap, plastic spoons, piece of nylon, Styrofoam, or a comb

Steps to Complete
1. Follow the directions found on *More Mudpies to Magnets* pg. 70.

Student Diary Assignment
- ☐ With the students, fill out the demonstration sheet found on SD pg. 45.

Nature Study: Weather Observation

This week, you are studying electricity. Storms have a very noticeable form of electricity: lightning. So, for your nature study this week, you will do another weather observation, but this time you will be specifically looking for storms.

Preparation
- Read the pp. 798-799 in the *Handbook of Nature Study* to learn more about storms.

Outdoor Time
- If you are able, observe a storm with lightning from inside your house. If not, watch the following video of lightning on YouTube:
  - http://www.youtube.com/watch?v=jiKNisWj-Hs
- Discuss what you see using the information you have learned from reading the *Handbook of Nature Study* to answer their questions or to share information about what they are observing.

Student Diary Assignment
- ☐ With the students, fill out the nature journal sheet found on SD pg. 47. The students can sketch what they have seen or you can write down their observations.

Read-Alouds

Optional Encyclopedia Pages
- *The Usborne Children's Encyclopedia* pp. 210-212 (Electricity)

Optional Library Books

📖 *The Magic School Bus and the Electric Field Trip* by Joanna Cole

Coordinating Activities

These following activities will help you to reinforce the week's topic and main idea.

- ✂ Art – (Dancing Electrons) Provide paper, glue, a paint brush, and silver glitter in a shaker for the students. Have them begin by painting glue on the paper. Next, have them shake glitter on their paper. Then, have them bounce the paper to make their electrons dance and settle on the glue!

    Student Diary Assignment
    📄 Have the students use SD pg. 46 to complete this activity.

    Lapbook Assignment
    📁 Have the students add the page they painted to the "My Physics Projects" pocket in the lapbook.

- ✂ Snack – (Lifesavers) This is not really a snack food, but real Wintergreen Lifesavers will spark when bitten into, which is fun and interesting for the student to see.

- ✂ More Fun – (Flying Hair) Have the students use static electricity to make hair "fly." You will need to rub a balloon on a shirt, just like you did for the introduction. Then, put the charged balloon near the student's hair and watch what static electricity can do!

Notes

Possible Schedules for Week 4

Two Days a Week Schedule	
Day 1	Day 2
❑ Read the introduction with the students. Color the main idea page. ❑ Complete the Hands-on Project "Static Electricity Tester" and fill out the demonstration sheet.	❑ Complete the Hands-on Project: Nature Study "Weather Observation" and fill out the nature journal sheet. ❑ Do the "Dancing Electrons" activity.
Supplies Needed for the Week ✓ Day 1: Balloon, Cotton shirt, Cork, String, Pin, Metallic paint, Glue, Static electricity producing objects (wool, rabbit fur, plastic wrap, plastic spoons, piece of nylon, Styrofoam, or a comb) ✓ Day 2: Paper, Glue, Paint brush, Silver glitter	

Five Days a Week Schedule				
Day 1	Day 2	Day 3	Day 4	Day 5
❑ Read the introduction with the students. Color the main idea page. ❑ Eat "Lifesavers" for snack.	❑ Complete the Hands-on Project "Static Electricity Tester" and fill out the demonstration sheet. ❑ Read the selected pages in *The Usborne Children's Encyclopedia*.	❑ Have some more fun with the "Flying Hair" activity. ❑ Complete the Static Electricity Mini-book. ❑ Choose one of the books from the read-aloud suggestions and read it to the students.	❑ Do the "Dancing Electrons" activity. ❑ Choose one of the books from the read-aloud suggestions and read it to the students.	❑ Complete the Hands-on Project: Nature Study "Weather Observation" and fill out the nature journal sheet.
Supplies Needed for the Week ✓ Day 1: Balloon, Cotton shirt, Wintergreen Lifesaver ✓ Day 2: Cork, String, Pin, Metallic paint, Glue, Static electricity producing objects (wool, rabbit fur, plastic wrap, plastic spoons, piece of nylon, Styrofoam, or a comb) ✓ Day 3: Balloon, Cotton shirt ✓ Day 4: Paper, Glue, Paint brush, Silver glitter				

Pulleys ~ Week 5

Weekly Topic

Main Idea
- Pulleys can help you lift a heavy load.

Introduction

Have several pictures of pulleys from the Internet or from a book. Say to the students:

Imagine we have a heavy box full of books that none of us can lift, but we needed to move it or we would lose the books.

? *How do you think we could lift it?*

Allow the student to share their ideas. Then, say to the student:

Those are great ideas! Another way to lift a heavy load would be to use a pulley like these.

Show the student the pictures of the pulleys and let them observe the images. Then, say to the student:

Pulleys are designed to help people lift a heavy load. Pulleys are simple machines that distribute the weight and multiply the pulling power, making it easier for a heavy load to be lifted up.

This week, we are going to spend some time looking at pulleys.

Student Diary Assignment
- Have the students color the coloring page found on SD pg. 48.

Lapbook Assignment
- Have the students cut out and color the Pulleys Mini-book on LT pg. 21. You can have them cut out the main idea graphic included and glue it in the interior of the mini-book or you can write a sentence with what they have learned from the week for them on the inside of the mini-book. Once the students are done, have them glue the booklet into the mini-lapbook.

Hands-on Projects

Scientific Demonstration: Pulley Things Along

In this demonstration, you will help the students to see how pulleys can be used.

Materials Needed
- 2 Spools of thread
- 2 Coat hangers
- String
- Small basket

Steps to Complete
1. Follow the directions found on *More Mudpies to Magnets* pg. 72.

Student Diary Assignment
- With the students, fill out the demonstration sheet found on SD pg. 49.

Nature Study: Ants

This week, you are studying pulleys which can help you lift heavy loads. Ants are known for their strength and can carry many times what they weigh. It's a bit of a stretch, but ants are going to be the focus of your nature study this week.

Preparation
- Read the pp. 369-372 in the *Handbook of Nature Study* to learn more about ants.

Outdoor Time
- Go on a walk with the students to look for ants. Allow the students to make observations about the ants. You can use the information you have learned from reading the *Handbook of Nature Study* to answer their questions or to share information about what they are observing.

Student Diary Assignment
- With the students, fill out the nature journal sheet found on SD pg. 51. The students can sketch what they have seen or you can write down their observations.

Read-Alouds

Optional Encyclopedia Pages
- *The Usborne Children's Encyclopedia* - There are no new pages scheduled.

Optional Library Books
- *Pull, Lift, and Lower: A Book About Pulleys* (Amazing Science: Simple Machines) by Dahl
- *What Is a Pulley?* (Welcome Books) by Lloyd G. Douglas

Coordinating Activities

These following activities will help you to reinforce the week's topic and main idea.

- **Art** – (Model Pulley) Beforehand, cut out 3 circles from black construction paper and one square from brown construction paper. Give the students the circles and the square, along with a piece of thin string. Have them make their own pulley design. Feel free to give them some guidance so that they create a pulley system that would actually work.

  Student Diary Assignment
  - Have the students use SD pg. 50 to complete this activity.

  Lapbook Assignment
  - Have the students add the page they painted to the "My Physics Projects" pocket in the lapbook.

- **Snack** – (Oreo Pulleys) Give the students several Oreo cookies and a long piece of licorice rope. Have them design a pulley on their plate, and then eat it!
- **More Fun** – (Develop a pulley system) Directions for this activity can be found in the want to do more section of pg. 72 in *More Mudpies to Magnets*. You will need the pulley you created for the hands-on project.

Notes

Possible Schedules for Week 5

Two Days a Week Schedule	
Day 1	Day 2
❏ Read the introduction with the students. Color the main idea page. ❏ Complete the Hands-on Project "Pulley Things Along" and fill out the demonstration sheet.	❏ Complete the Hands-on Project: Nature Study "Ants" and fill out the nature journal sheet. ❏ Do the "Model Pulley" activity.
Supplies Needed for the Week ✓ Day 1: Pictures of pulleys, 2 Spools of thread, 2 Coat hangers, String, Small basket ✓ Day 2: Black and brown construction paper, String, Glue	

Five Days a Week Schedule				
Day 1	Day 2	Day 3	Day 4	Day 5
❏ Read the introduction with the students. Color the main idea page. ❏ Eat "Oreo Pulleys" for snack.	❏ Complete the Hands-on Project "Pulley Things Along" and fill out the demonstration sheet. ❏ Choose one of the books from the read-aloud suggestions and read it to the students.	❏ Have some more fun with the "Develop a pulley system" activity. ❏ Complete the Pulleys Mini-book.	❏ Do the "Model Pulley" activity. ❏ Choose one of the books from the read-aloud suggestions and read it to the students.	❏ Complete the Hands-on Project: Nature Study "Ants" and fill out the nature journal sheet.
Supplies Needed for the Week ✓ Day 1: Pictures of pulleys, Oreo cookies, Licorice rope ✓ Day 2: 2 Spools of thread, 2 Coat hangers, String, Small basket ✓ Day 3: Pulley from the Hands-on Project on Day 2 ✓ Day 4: Black and brown construction paper, String, Glue				

Light ~ Week 6

Weekly Topic

Main Idea

- Light is the type of energy that helps us to see.

Introduction

If possible, share this introduction while you are in a room with no windows. Start with the lights on. Say to the students:

When the lights are on in a room, we can see a lot of things.

? *What do you see in this room?*

Let the students look around and take time to answer your question. Then, say:

Those are good observations. But if the lights aren't on, it is much harder for us to see the objects in the room.

If the students are afraid of the dark, skip the next question. If the students are not afraid of the dark, turn off the lights and ask the following question:

? *What do you see now?*

Let the students look around and take time to answer your question. Then, turn back on the lights and say:

It is a lot harder for us to see the things in the room when the lights are out. This is because light helps us to see. Light is actually a type of energy that helps us to see.

This week, we are going to look closer at light.

Student Diary Assignment

- Have the students color the coloring page found on SD pg. 52.

Lapbook Assignment

- Have the students cut out and color the Light Mini-book on LT pg. 22. You can have them cut out the main idea graphic included and glue it in the interior of the mini-book or you can write a sentence with what they have learned from the week for them on the inside of the mini-book. Once the students are done, have them glue the booklet into the mini-lapbook.

Hands-on Projects

Scientific Demonstration: The Reflection Direction

In this demonstration, you will help the students to see how light can be reflected.

Materials Needed
- Flat mirror
- Flashlight
- Tennis ball

Steps to Complete
1. Follow the directions found on *More Mudpies to Magnets* pg. 76."

Student Diary Assignment
- With the students, fill out the demonstration sheet found on SD pg. 53.

Nature Study: The Sun

This week, you are going to look at the sun, our source of natural light during the day. (*Note* – *You will look at the sun again in the first week of the Meteorology unit.*)

Preparation
- Read the pp. 833-834 in the *Handbook of Nature Study* to learn more about the Sun.

Outdoor Time
- Go on a walk with the students to feel the power of the Sun. Allow the students to observe the difference between being in the sun and being in the shade. You can use the information you have learned from reading the *Handbook of Nature Study* to answer their questions or to share information about what they are observing.

Student Diary Assignment
- With the students, fill out the nature journal sheet found on SD pg. 55. The students can sketch what they have seen or you can write down their observations.

Read-Alouds

Optional Encyclopedia Pages
- *The Usborne Children's Encyclopedia* pp. 192-193 (Energy)

Optional Library Books

- *All About Light* (Rookie Read-About Science) by Lisa Trumbauer
- *Exploring Light* (How Does Science Work?) by Carol Ballard
- *The Magic School Bus: Gets A Bright Idea, The: A Book About Light* by Nancy White

Coordinating Activities

These following activities will help you to reinforce the week's topic and main idea.

- **Art** – (My Reflection Collage) Go on a hunt for reflective materials in your house or provide the students with a collection of reflective materials they can use to make their collage. Have them glue the various materials on a sheet of paper and then take it outside to see how the collage reflects the light.

  Student Diary Assignment
  - Have the students use SD pg. 54 to complete this activity.

  Lapbook Assignment
  - Have the students add the page they painted to the "My Physics Projects" pocket in the lapbook.

- **Game** – (Play Flashlight tag) Use the same rules you would for a game a tag, except the person must be "touched" by a beam of light before they are "it." The person who is "it" has the flashlight.

Notes

Possible Schedules for Week 6

Two Days a Week Schedule	
Day 1	Day 2
❏ Read the introduction with the students. Color the main idea page. ❏ Complete the Hands-on Project "Reflection Direction" and fill out the demonstration sheet.	❏ Complete the Hands-on Project: Nature Study "The Sun" and fill out the nature journal sheet. ❏ Do the "My Reflective Collage" activity.
Supplies Needed for the Week ✓ Day 1: Flat mirror, Flashlight, Tennis ball ✓ Day 2: Reflective materials, Paper, Glue	

Five Days a Week Schedule				
Day 1	Day 2	Day 3	Day 4	Day 5
❏ Read the introduction with the students. Color the main idea page. ❏ Choose one of the books from the read-aloud suggestions and read it to the students.	❏ Complete the Hands-on Project "Reflection Direction" and fill out the demonstration sheet. ❏ Read the selected pages in *The Usborne Children's Encyclopedia*.	❏ Play a game of "Flashlight Tag." ❏ Complete the Light Mini-book.	❏ Do the "My Reflective Collage" activity. ❏ Choose one of the books from the read-aloud suggestions and read it to the students.	❏ Complete the Hands-on Project: Nature Study "The Sun" and fill out the nature journal sheet.
Supplies Needed for the Week ✓ Day 2: Flat mirror, Flashlight, Tennis ball ✓ Day 3: Flashlights ✓ Day 4: Reflective materials, Paper, Glue				

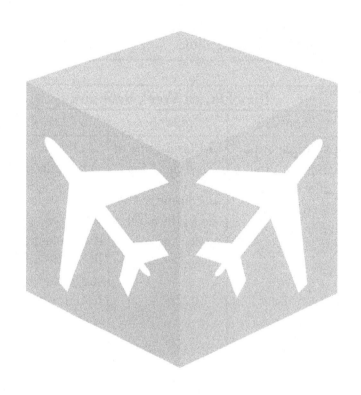

Intro to Science
Unit 3: Intro to Geology

Intro to Geology Unit Overview

Sequence for Study
- Week 1: Fossils
- Week 2: Rocks
- Week 3: Metamorphic Rock
- Week 4: Volcanoes
- Week 5: Sedimentary Rock
- Week 6: Compass

Supplies Needed for the Unit

Week	Introduction Props	Hands-on Project Materials	Coordinating Activities Supplies
1	Several pictures of fossils (or an actual fossil)	Soil, Water, Wax paper, Cookie sheet, Container, Small objects, Fossil rock	Sugar cookie dough, Several plant or animal stamps or stencils, Gray or brown paint, Paper
2	Several rocks from your area	Rocks, Dried grass, Leaves, Sticks, Egg carton, Magnifying glass	Rock candy, Several rocks you have collected, Several colors of paint, Medium sized rock
3	Several metamorphic rocks	Plastic cups, White vinegar, Several types of rocks, including limestone or chalk, Metamorphic rocks	Peanut butter (or other nut butter), jelly, bread, Plastic cups, White vinegar, Several types of rocks, including limestone or chalk, Crayons, Paper, Cardboard, Hair dryer
4	*No supplies needed.*	Soup can, Vinegar, Water, Baking soda, Red food coloring, Clay, sand, soil or leaves, Igneous rock	Plastic yogurt container, Scissors, Toothpaste, Dirt, Paint (black, gray, orange, red), Paper
5	Sandstone	Pint jar, Muddy water, Sand, Rocks, 2-Liter soda bottle, Sedimentary rock	Graham crackers Peanut butter, Sugar, Mini chocolate chips, Sand, Glue, Pebbles, Bread loaf pan, Plastic wrap, Paint, Sand, Paper
6	Compass, Map	Compass, Signs for north, south, east, and west, Chalk	Sugar cookies, Icing, Pencil, Paper

Books Scheduled

Hands-on Projects (Required Books)
- *More Mudpies to Magnets* (If you are using the scientific demonstration option.)
- *Handbook of Nature Study* (If you are using the nature study option.)

Read-Aloud Suggestions

Optional Encyclopedia
- *The Usborne Children's Encyclopedia*

Week 1
- *Mary Anning: Fossil Hunter* by Sally M. Walker and Phyllis V. Saroff
- *Viewfinder: Fossils* by Douglas Palmer and Neil D. L. Clark
- *What Do You Know About Fossils?* (20 Questions: Science) by Suzanne Slade
- *Fossils Tell of Long Ago* (Let's-Read-and-Find Out Science 2) by Aliki

Week 2
- *Looking at Rocks* (My First Field Guides) by Jennifer Dussling and Tim Haggerty
- *Rocks: Hard, Soft, Smooth, and Rough* (Amazing Science) by Rosinsky, Natalie M, John, and Matthew
- *Rocks and Fossils* (Science Kids) by Chris Pellant
- *Rocks! Rocks! Rocks!* by Nancy Elizabeth Wallace

Week 3
- *Metamorphic Rocks* (Earth Rocks!) by Holly Cefrey
- *I Love Rocks* (Rookie Readers, Level B) by Cari Meister and Terry Sirrell

Week 4
- *National Geographic Readers: Volcanoes!* by Anne Schreiber
- *Jump into Science: Volcano!* by Ellen J. Prager and Nancy Woodman
- *Volcanoes* (Let's-Read-and-Find... Science 2) by Franklyn M. Branley and Megan Lloyd
- *The Magic School Bus Blows Its Top: A Book About Volcanoes* (Magic School Bus) by Gail Herman and Bob Ostrom

Week 5
- *Sedimentary Rocks* (Earth Rocks!) by Holly Cefrey
- *Earthsteps: A Rock's Journey through Time* by Diane Nelson Spickert and Marianne D. Wallace

Week 6
- *You Can Use a Compass* (Rookie Read-About Science) by Lisa Trumbauer
- *North, South, East, and West* (Rookie Read-About Science) by Allan Fowler
- *Maps and Globes* by Jack Knowlton and Harriet Barton

Fossils ~ Week 1

Weekly Topic

Main Idea
- Fossils are imprints of long-gone plants or animals.

Introduction

Have several pictures of fossils from books and magazines (or have several rocks with fossils) on the table in front of you. As you show the pictures to the students, say:

This is a fossil. We find fossils in rocks all over the Earth.

They are the remains of plants or animals that died many years ago. When they died, they got stuck in the mud and as time went by, more mud pressed on top of them.

Eventually, there was so much weight that the mud turned into rock and the impression of the plant or animal was stuck in it.

? *Can you find the plant or animal impression in these fossil pictures?*

Give them time to observe the pictures (or fossils) before you say:

This week, we are going to look closer at fossils.

Student Diary Assignment
- Have the students color the coloring page found on SD pg. 58.

Lapbook Assignment
- Have the students cut out and color the Fossils Mini-book on LT pg. 27. You can have them cut out the main idea graphic included and glue it in the interior of the mini-book or you can write a sentence with what they have learned from the week for them on the inside of the mini-book. Once the students are done, have them glue the booklet into the mini-lapbook.

Hands-on Projects

Scientific Demonstration: Stir-in fossils

In this demonstration, you will help the students to see how fossils are made.

Materials Needed
- ✓ Soil
- ✓ Water
- ✓ Wax paper
- ✓ Cookie sheet
- ✓ Container
- ✓ Small objects (such as sea shells, pieces of wood, leaves, rocks, nuts in shells)

Steps to Complete
1. Follow the directions found on *More Mudpies to Magnets* pg. 87.

Student Diary Assignment
- ☐ With the students, fill out the demonstration sheet found on SD pg. 59.

Nature Study: Fossil Find

This week, you are looking for fossils in nature. Although there are places that are easier to find fossils, fossils can be found anywhere. If fossils are not easy to find in your area, have a piece on hand to observe.

Preparation
- Read the pp. 756-757 in the *Handbook of Nature Study* to learn more about fossils.

Outdoor Time
- Go on a walk with the students to look for fossils. Allow the students to make observations about any fossils they find. You can use the information you have learned from reading the *Handbook of Nature Study* to answer their questions or to share information about what they are observing.

Student Diary Assignment
- ☐ With the students, fill out the nature journal sheet found on SD pg. 61. The students can sketch what they have seen or you can write down their observations.

Read-Alouds

Optional Encyclopedia Pages
- *The Usborne Children's Encyclopedia* pg. 19 (Fossils)

Optional Library Books
- *Mary Anning: Fossil Hunter* by Sally M. Walker and Phyllis V. Saroff

- *Viewfinder: Fossils* by Douglas Palmer and Neil D. L. Clark
- *What Do You Know About Fossils?* (20 Questions: Science) by Suzanne Slade
- *Fossils Tell of Long Ago* (Let's-Read-and-Find Out Science 2) by Aliki

Coordinating Activities

These following activities will help you to reinforce the week's topic and main idea.

- **Art** – (Fossil Prints) Beforehand, collect several stamps or stencils that have a leaf, starfish, or other small plant or animal on it. Begin by having the students paint gray or brown paint on a sheet of paper. Then, have the students use the stamps or stencils with black paint to make fossils in their rocks.

  Student Diary Assignment
  - Have the students use SD pg. 60 to complete this activity.

  Lapbook Assignment
  - Have the students cut out the "My Geology Projects" pocket on LT pg. 33. Have them glue the pocket into the lapbook and add the painting project they just did to the pocket.

- **Snack** – (Fossil Cookies) Make your favorite sugar cookie dough recipe. Have you student make rocks out of the cookies and then using forks, spoon, knives, or fingers, create create fossils on the cookies.

Notes

Possible Schedules for Week 1

Two Days a Week Schedule	
Day 1	Day 2
❏ Read the introduction with the students. Color the main idea page. ❏ Complete the Hands-on Project "Stir-in Fossils" and fill out the demonstration sheet.	❏ Complete the Hands-on Project: Nature Study "Fossil Find" and fill out the nature journal sheet. ❏ Do the "Fossil Prints" activity.
Supplies Needed for the Week ✓ Day 1: Several pictures of fossils (or an actual fossil), Soil, Water, Wax paper, Cookie sheet, Container, Small objects ✓ Day 2: Several plant or animal stamps or stencils, Gray or brown paint, Paper	

Five Days a Week Schedule				
Day 1	Day 2	Day 3	Day 4	Day 5
❏ Read the introduction with the students. Color the main idea page. ❏ Eat "Fossil Cookies" for snack.	❏ Complete the Hands-on Project "Stir-in Fossils" and fill out the demonstration sheet. ❏ Read the selected page in *The Usborne Children's Encyclopedia*.	❏ Complete the Fossils Mini-book. ❏ Choose one of the books from the read-aloud suggestions and read it to the students.	❏ Do the "Fossil Prints" activity. ❏ Choose one of the books from the read-aloud suggestions and read it to the students.	❏ Complete the Hands-on Project: Nature Study "Fossil Find" and fill out the nature journal sheet.
Supplies Needed for the Week ✓ Day 1: Several pictures of fossils (or an actual fossil), Sugar cookie dough ✓ Day 2: Soil, Water, Wax paper, Cookie sheet, Container, Small objects ✓ Day 4: Several plant or animal stamps or stencils, Gray or brown paint, Paper ✓ Day 5: Fossils				

Rocks ~ Week 2

Weekly Topic

Main Idea
- There are many different types of rocks.

Introduction
Have several rocks from your area on the table in front of you. Say to the students:

There are many different types of rocks and they have many different uses. Rocks are used to build buildings, to form statues and to create clay pots.

We can find rocks almost anywhere. These are several of the types of rocks you can find where we live.

? *What do you notice about these rocks?*

Give them time to observe the rocks before you say:

This week, we are going to spend some time collecting and looking at rocks.

If you have a rock field guide on hand, give the students some time to look through the guide.

Student Diary Assignment
- Have the students color the coloring page found on SD pg. 62.

Lapbook Assignment
- Have the students cut out and color the Rocks Mini-book on LT pg. 28. You can have them cut out the main idea graphic included and glue it in the interior of the mini-book or you can write a sentence with what they have learned from the week for them on the inside of the mini-book. Once the students are done, have them glue the booklet into the mini-lapbook.

Hands-on Projects

Scientific Demonstration: Pet Rocks on Parade

In this demonstration, you will help the students a chance to showcase their rocks.

Materials Needed
- ✓ Rocks

- ✓ Dried grass
- ✓ Leaves
- ✓ Sticks
- ✓ Egg carton
- ✓ Magnifying glass

Steps to Complete
1. Follow the directions found on *More Mudpies to Magnets* pg. 88.

Student Diary Assignment
- ☐ With the students, fill out the demonstration sheet found on SD pg. 63.

Nature Study: Rock Hunt

This week, you are looking for rocks in nature.

Preparation
- Read the pp. 743-745 in the *Handbook of Nature Study* to learn more about rocks.

Outdoor Time
- Go on a walk with the students to look for rocks. Allow the students to make observations about any rocks they find. You can use the information you have learned from reading the *Handbook of Nature Study* to answer their questions or to share information about what they are observing.

Student Diary Assignment
- ☐ With the students, fill out the nature journal sheet found on SD pg. 65. The students can sketch what they have seen or you can write down their observations.

Read-Alouds

Optional Encyclopedia Pages
- *The Usborne Children's Encyclopedia* pg. 18 Rocks

Optional Library Books
- *Looking at Rocks* (My First Field Guides) by Jennifer Dussling and Tim Haggerty
- *Rocks: Hard, Soft, Smooth, and Rough* (Amazing Science) by Rosinsky, Natalie M, John, and Matthew
- *Rocks and Fossils* (Science Kids) by Chris Pellant
- *Rocks! Rocks! Rocks!* by Nancy Elizabeth Wallace

Coordinating Activities

These following activities will help you to reinforce the week's topic and main idea.

- ✂ Art – (Painting Rocks) Give the students several colors of paint and a medium sized rock that they have collected. Let them choose the design they want to paint on the rock.

  Student Diary Assignment
  - 🗒 Have the students take a picture or their rock and have the students glue a picture of their painted rock on SD pg. 64 to complete this activity.

  Lapbook Assignment
  - 📂 Have the students take a picture of their rock and add the photo to the "My Geology Projects" pocket in the lapbook.

- ✂ Snack – (Rock Candy) Get some rock candy to eat for snack or make your own using the recipe in the Appendix pg. 187.
- ✂ More Fun – (Classifying Rocks) Using a rock field guide or the Internet, classify the rocks you have collected. You will need to heavily guide the students through this activity.

Notes

Possible Schedules for Week 2

Two Days a Week Schedule	
Day 1	Day 2
❑ Read the introduction with the students. Color the main idea page. ❑ Complete the Hands-on Project "Pet Rocks on Parade" and fill out the demonstration sheet.	❑ Complete the Hands-on Project: Nature Study "Rock Hunt" and fill out the nature journal sheet. ❑ Do the "Painting Rocks" activity.
Supplies Needed for the Week ✓ Day 1: Several rocks from your area, Rocks, Dried grass, Leaves, Sticks, Egg carton, Magnifying glass ✓ Day 2: Several colors of paint, Medium sized rock	

Five Days a Week Schedule				
Day 1	Day 2	Day 3	Day 4	Day 5
❑ Read the introduction with the students. Color the main idea page. ❑ Eat "Rock Candy" for snack.	❑ Complete the Hands-on Project "Pet Rocks on Parade" and fill out the demonstration sheet. ❑ Read the selected page in *The Usborne Children's Encyclopedia*.	❑ Have some more fun with the "Classifying Rocks" activity. ❑ Complete the Rocks Mini-book. ❑ Choose one of the books from the read-aloud suggestions and read it to the students.	❑ Do the "Painting Rocks" activity. ❑ Choose one of the books from the read-aloud suggestions and read it to the students.	❑ Complete the Hands-on Project: Nature Study "Rock Hunt" and fill out the nature journal sheet.
Supplies Needed for the Week ✓ Day 1: Several rocks from your area, rock candy ✓ Day 2: Rocks, Dried grass, Leaves, Sticks, Egg carton, Magnifying glass ✓ Day 3: Several rocks you have collected ✓ Day 4: Several colors of paint, Medium sized rock				

84

Metamorphic Rock ~ Week 3

Weekly Topic

Main Idea
- Metamorphic rocks are rocks that have changed.

Introduction
Have several metamorphic rocks (marble, granite, limestone, or slate are good examples) on the table in front of you. Say to the students:

Metamorphic rocks are a special type of rock that has been changed by heat and pressure.

These rocks start out as layers of dead organic material or bits of other rocks, which are smushed into sedimentary rock. Then, over time, the sedimentary rock is pressed and smashed to form metamorphic rock. So, by the time a rock becomes metamorphic rock, it has undergone several changes.

Pick up one of the rocks from the table and ask:

? *What do you notice about this rock?*

Give them time to observe all of the rocks before you say:

This week, we are going to look closer at different types of metamorphic rock.

Student Diary Assignment
- Have the students color the coloring page found on SD pg. 66.

Lapbook Assignment
- Have the students cut out and color the Metamorphic Rock Mini-book on LT pg. 29. You can have them cut out the main idea graphic included and glue it in the interior of the mini-book or you can write a sentence with what they have learned from the week for them on the inside of the mini-book. Once the students are done, have them glue the booklet into the mini-lapbook.

Hands-on Projects

Scientific Demonstration: The Acid Test

In this demonstration, you will help the students to see how see how scientist can test for the presence of metamorphic rock.

Materials Needed
- ✓ Plastic cups
- ✓ White vinegar
- ✓ Several types of rocks, including limestone or chalk

Steps to Complete
1. Follow the directions found on *More Mudpies to Magnets* pg. 89.

Student Diary Assignment
- ☐ With the students, fill out the demonstration sheet found on SD pg. 67.

Nature Study: Metamorphic Rock

This week, you are looking for metamorphic rocks in nature. If metamorphic rocks are not easy to find in your area, have a piece on hand to observe.

Preparation
- Read the pp. 748-749 in the *Handbook of Nature Study* to learn more about metamorphic rock.

Outdoor Time
- Go on a walk with the students to look for calcite, granite, slate, limestone, or marble. Allow the students to make observations about what they find. You can use the information you have learned from reading the *Handbook of Nature Study* to answer their questions or to share information about what they are observing.

Student Diary Assignment
- ☐ With the students, fill out the nature journal sheet found on SD pg. 69. The students can sketch what they have seen or you can write down their observations.

Read-Alouds

Optional Encyclopedia Pages
- *The Usborne Children's Encyclopedia* - There are no new pages scheduled.

Optional Library Books
- *Metamorphic Rocks* (Earth Rocks!) by Holly Cefrey
- *I Love Rocks* (Rookie Readers, Level B) by Cari Meister and Terry Sirrell

Coordinating Activities

These following activities will help you to reinforce the week's topic and main idea.

- **Art** – (Metamorphic Art) Let the students choose three to five crayons that they love and hand them to you. Set a sheet of paper on a piece of cardboard and set the crayons at the end of a sheet of paper. Using a hair dryer, gently apply heat to the crayons so that the wax melts and spreads up the sheet of paper. Let the designs completely cool before you let the students touch the designs.

    Student Diary Assignment
    - Have the students use SD pg. 68 to complete this activity.

    Lapbook Assignment
    - Have the students add their art to the "My Geology Projects" pocket in the lapbook.

- **Snack** – (Metamorphic Rock Sandwich) Make a peanut butter and jelly sandwich, using chunky peanut butter. (*Note – If the students are allergic to peanuts, use another nut butter with a few chopped seeds or nuts sprinkled on top*.) Cut it in half and set one half of the sandwich aside. (*This is your sedimentary rock sandwich-rock formed layer by layer.*) Then take the other half and apply pressure. (*This is your metamorphic rock sandwich-rock that is formed when the layers of sedimentary rock are put under pressure.*) Taste both sandwiches and talk about the differences between them.

Notes

Possible Schedules for Week 3

Two Days a Week Schedule	
Day 1	Day 2
❑ Read the introduction with the students. Color the main idea page. ❑ Complete the Hands-on Project "The Acid Test" and fill out the demonstration sheet.	❑ Complete the Hands-on Project: Nature Study "Metamorphic Rock" and fill out the nature journal sheet. ❑ Do the "Metamorphic Art" activity.
Supplies Needed for the Week ✓ Day 1: Several metamorphic rocks, Plastic cups, White vinegar, Several types of rocks, including limestone or chalk ✓ Day 2: Crayons, Paper, Cardboard, Hair dryer	

Five Days a Week Schedule				
Day 1	Day 2	Day 3	Day 4	Day 5
❑ Read the introduction with the students. Color the main idea page. ❑ Eat "Metamorphic Rock Sandwich" for snack.	❑ Complete the Hands-on Project "The Acid Test" and fill out the demonstration sheet.	❑ Complete the Metamorphic Rock Mini-book. ❑ Choose one of the books from the read-aloud suggestions and read it to the students.	❑ Do the "Metamorphic Art" activity. ❑ Choose one of the books from the read-aloud suggestions and read it to the students.	❑ Complete the Hands-on Project: Nature Study "Metamorphic Rock" and fill out the nature journal sheet.
Supplies Needed for the Week ✓ Day 1: Several metamorphic rocks, Peanut butter (or other nut butter), jelly, bread ✓ Day 2: Plastic cups, White vinegar, Several types of rocks, including limestone or chalk ✓ Day 4: Crayons, Paper, Cardboard, Hair dryer ✓ Day 5: Metamorphic rocks				

Volcano ~ Week 4

Weekly Topic

Main Idea
- Volcanoes explode hot, sticky rock from inside the Earth.

Introduction
Say to the students:

Volcanoes are found all over the world, including under the sea.

The center of a volcano is filled with hot rock, called magma, which comes from deep inside the Earth. When the magma gets too hot, pressure builds up and eventually the volcano blows its top!

When this happens, it spills out ash and hot, sticky rock, which we call lava. This week, we are going to make our own volcano and have a pretend explosion!

If you would like to show your students a bit more about Hawaii's volcanoes, we recommend watching the following video together:

- https://www.youtube.com/watch?v=uhZTZShA1dc

Student Diary Assignment
- Have the students color the coloring page found on SD pg. 70.

Lapbook Assignment
- Have the students cut out and color the Volcanoes Mini-book on LT pg. 30. You can have them cut out the main idea graphic included and glue it in the interior of the mini-book or you can write a sentence with what they have learned from the week for them on the inside of the mini-book. Once the students are done, have them glue the booklet into the mini-lapbook.

Hands-on Projects

Scientific Demonstration: Instant Volcano

In this demonstration, you will help the students to see how a volcano explodes.

Materials Needed
- Soup can

- ✓ Vinegar
- ✓ Water
- ✓ Baking soda
- ✓ Red food coloring
- ✓ Clay, sand, soil or leaves

Steps to Complete
1. Follow the directions found on *More Mudpies to Magnets* pg. 91.

Student Diary Assignment
- ☐ With the students, fill out the demonstration sheet found on SD pg. 71.

Nature Study: Igneous Rock

This week, you are studying volcanoes. Igneous rocks are rocks formed by volcanoes, so they will be the focus of your nature study this week. If igneous rocks are not easy to find in your area, have a piece on hand to observe.

Preparation
- Read the pp. 746-747 in the *Handbook of Nature Study* to learn more about igneous rock.

Outdoor Time
- ☼ Go on a walk with the students to look for igneous rocks. Allow the students to make observations about what they find. You can use the information you have learned from reading the *Handbook of Nature Study* to answer their questions or to share information about what they are observing.

Student Diary Assignment
- ☐ With the students, fill out the nature journal sheet found on SD pg. 73. The students can sketch what they have seen or you can write down their observations.

Read-Alouds

Optional Encyclopedia Pages
- *The Usborne Children's Encyclopedia* - There are no new pages scheduled.

Optional Library Books
- *National Geographic Readers: Volcanoes!* by Anne Schreiber
- *Jump into Science: Volcano!* by Ellen J. Prager and Nancy Woodman
- *Volcanoes* (Let's-Read-and-Find... Science 2) by Franklyn M. Branley and Megan

Lloyd

📖 *The Magic School Bus Blows Its Top: A Book About Volcanoes* (Magic School Bus) by Gail Herman and Bob Ostrom

Coordinating Activities

These following activities will help you to reinforce the week's topic and main idea.

✂ **Art** – (My Volcano) Give the students some black, gray, orange, and red paint. Have them paint their own volcano on a sheet of paper. You can also add some texture to their volcano by adding salt or cornstarch to the paint.

Student Diary Assignment
 ▢ Have the students use SD pg. 72 to complete this activity.

Lapbook Assignment
 📁 Have the students add their volcano to the "My Geology Projects" pocket in the lapbook.

✂ **More Fun** – (Toothpaste Volcano) Use a pair of scissors or a knife to cut a hole large enough to fit the tip of a toothpaste tube on the bottom of an empty plastic yogurt container. Remove the cap from a toothpaste tube and insert it in the hole you just cut. Have the student help you fill the yogurt container about two-thirds of the way full with dirt and pack it down. Then, have them squeeze the toothpaste tube and see what happens! (*The toothpaste will "erupt" out of the dirt, but it can take a bit of effort to make that happen.*)

Notes

Possible Schedules for Week 4

Two Days a Week Schedule	
Day 1	Day 2
❏ Read the introduction with the students. Color the main idea page. ❏ Complete the Hands-on Project "Instant Volcano" and fill out the demonstration sheet.	❏ Complete the Hands-on Project: Nature Study "Igneous Rock" and fill out the nature journal sheet. ❏ Do the "My Volcano" activity.
Supplies Needed for the Week ✓ Day 1: Soup can, Vinegar, Water, Baking soda, Red food coloring, Clay, sand, soil or leaves ✓ Day 2: Igneous rock, Paint (black, gray, orange, red), Paper	

Five Days a Week Schedule				
Day 1	Day 2	Day 3	Day 4	Day 5
❏ Read the introduction with the students. Color the main idea page. ❏ Watch the volcano video.	❏ Complete the Hands-on Project "Instant Volcano" and fill out the demonstration sheet. ❏ Choose one of the books from the read-aloud suggestions and read it to the students.	❏ Have some more fun with the "Toothpaste Volcano" activity. ❏ Complete the Volcano Mini-book.	❏ Do the "My Volcano" activity. ❏ Choose one of the books from the read-aloud suggestions and read it to the students.	❏ Complete the Hands-on Project: Nature Study "Igneous Rock" and fill out the nature journal sheet.
Supplies Needed for the Week ✓ Day 2: Soup can, Vinegar, Water, Baking soda, Red food coloring, Clay, sand, soil or leaves ✓ Day 3: Plastic yogurt container, Scissors, Toothpaste, Dirt ✓ Day 4: Paint (black, gray, orange, red), Paper ✓ Day 5: Igneous rock				

Sedimentary Rock ~ Week 5

Weekly Topic

Main Idea
- Sedimentary rock is made from layers of sand, mud, or pebbles.

Introduction
Have a piece of sandstone out on the table in front of you. Say to the students:

This is a piece of rock is called sandstone, which is a type of sedimentary rock. Sedimentary rock is formed layer by layer. As sand, mud, and pebbles settle, they build up and squeeze together to form rock.

? *Can you see the layers in this rock?*

? *How about the bits of sand?*

Give them time to observe all of the rocks before you say:

Those are good observations! This piece of sandstone was formed from lots and lots of layers of sand were pressed together over time. This week, we are going to look at sedimentary rocks.

Student Diary Assignment
- Have the students color the coloring page found on SD pg. 74.

Lapbook Assignment
- Have the students cut out and color the Sedimentary Rock Mini-book on LT pg. 31. You can have them cut out the main idea graphic included and glue it in the interior of the mini-book or you can write a sentence with what they have learned from the week for them on the inside of the mini-book. Once the students are done, have them glue the booklet into the mini-lapbook.

Hands-on Projects

Scientific Demonstration: Cleaning Muddy Water

In this demonstration, you will help the students to see how see how sand and sedimentary rock can be used for filtering water.

Materials Needed
- ✓ Pint jar
- ✓ Muddy water
- ✓ Sand
- ✓ Rocks
- ✓ 2-Liter soda bottle

Steps to Complete
1. Follow the directions found on *More Mudpies to Magnets* pg. 95.

Student Diary Assignment
- With the students, fill out the demonstration sheet found on SD pg. 75.

Nature Study: Sedimentary Rock

This week, you are looking for sedimentary rocks in nature. If sedimentary rocks are not easy to find in your area, have a piece on hand to observe.

Preparation
- Read the pg. 745 in the *Handbook of Nature Study* to learn more about sedimentary rock.

Outdoor Time
- Go on a walk with the students to look for sedimentary rocks. Allow the students to make observations about what they find. You can use the information you have learned from reading the *Handbook of Nature Study* to answer their questions or to share information about what they are observing.

Student Diary Assignment
- With the students, fill out the nature journal sheet found on SD pg. 77. The students can sketch what they have seen or you can write down their observations.

Read-Alouds

Optional Encyclopedia Pages
- *The Usborne Children's Encyclopedia* - There are no new pages scheduled.

Optional Library Books
- *Sedimentary Rocks* (Earth Rocks!) by Holly Cefrey
- *Earthsteps: A Rock's Journey through Time* by Diane Nelson Spickert and Marianne D. Wallace

Coordinating Activities

These following activities will help you to reinforce the week's topic and main idea.

- **Art** – (Sand Painting) Give the students some paint in the color of their choice and a bowl with sand in it. Have them mix the paint and sand together and then have the students use the sand paint to create a picture on a piece of paper.

    Student Diary Assignment
    - Have the students use SD pg. 76 to complete this activity.

    Lapbook Assignment
    - Have the students add the sand painting to the "My Geology Projects" pocket in the lapbook.

- **Snack** – (Sedimentary Cookies) Use graham crackers as a base, peanut butter (or other nut butter) for the mud, sugar for the sand and mini chocolate chips for the pebbles. Have your students layer their graham cracker with mud, sand, and pebbles, and top it with another graham cracker. Then, squeeze the layers together gently, just like sedimentary rock, eat, and enjoy.

- **More Fun** – (Make Sandstone) Have the students mix together 2 cups of sand and ½ cup of glue. You can also add a few pebbles in as well. Press this mixture into a bread loaf pan that has been lined with plastic wrap. Cover with plastic wrap and press as hard as you can to really squeeze the mixture together. Let it dry, and you will have your very own sandstone.

Notes

Possible Schedules for Week 5

Two Days a Week Schedule	
Day 1	Day 2
❑ Read the introduction with the students. Color the main idea page. ❑ Complete the Hands-on Project "Cleaning Muddy Water" and fill out the demonstration sheet.	❑ Complete the Hands-on Project: Nature Study "Sedimentary Rock" and fill out the nature journal sheet. ❑ Do the "Sand Painting" activity.
Supplies Needed for the Week ✓ Day 1: Sandstone, Pint jar, Muddy water, Sand, Rocks, 2-Liter soda bottle ✓ Day 2: Sedimentary rock, Paint, Sand, Paper	

Five Days a Week Schedule				
Day 1	Day 2	Day 3	Day 4	Day 5
❑ Read the introduction with the students. Color the main idea page. ❑ Eat "Sedimentary Cookies" for snack.	❑ Complete the Hands-on Project "Cleaning Muddy Water" and fill out the demonstration sheet. ❑ Choose one of the books from the read-aloud suggestions and read it to the students.	❑ Have some more fun with the "Make Sandstone" activity. ❑ Complete the Sedimentary Rock Mini-book.	❑ Do the "Sand Painting" activity. ❑ Choose one of the books from the read-aloud suggestions and read it to the students.	❑ Complete the Hands-on Project: Nature Study "Sedimentary Rock" and fill out the nature journal sheet.
Supplies Needed for the Week ✓ Day 1: Sandstone, Graham crackers Peanut butter, Sugar, Mini chocolate chips ✓ Day 2: Pint jar, Muddy water, Sand, Rocks, 2-Liter soda bottle ✓ Day 3: Sand, Glue, Pebbles, Bread loaf pan, Plastic wrap ✓ Day 4: Paint, Sand, Paper ✓ Day 5: Sedimentary rock				

Compass ~ Week 6

Weekly Topic

Main Idea
- A compass shows us north, south, east, and west.

Introduction

Have a compass and a map with a compass rose on it on the table in front of you. Say to the students:

This is a compass. We use it to tell us which direction we are going or to find where north is.

Let the students hold the compass and observe how it works. Then say:

Every map has a compass rose on it. The compass rose shows us where north, south, east, and west are on a map. This is so we can use a map of an area and a compass to guide you to where you want to go. This week, we are going to spend some more time learning about compasses and maps.

Student Diary Assignment
- Have the students color the coloring page found on SD pg. 78.

Lapbook Assignment
- Have the students cut out and color the Compass Mini-book on LT pg. 32. You can have them cut out the main idea graphic included and glue it in the interior of the mini-book or you can write a sentence with what they have learned from the week for them on the inside of the mini-book. Once the students are done, have them glue the booklet into the mini-lapbook.

Hands-on Projects

Scientific Demonstration: Head North, Child, North

In this demonstration, you will help the students to see how see how a compass works and where north is.

Materials Needed
- ✓ Compass

- ✓ Signs for north, south, east, and west
- ✓ Chalk

Steps to Complete
1. Follow the directions found on *More Mudpies to Magnets* pg. 93.

Student Diary Assignment
- ☐ With the students, fill out the demonstration sheet found on SD pg. 79.

Nature Study: Nature Map

This week, your students will practice using a compass and a map in their backyard.

Preparation
- ✏ Make a map of a path through your backyard, complete with natural landmarks and a compass rose. Write up directions using north, east, south, and west to give to the students so that they can use their compass to follow your map.

Outdoor Time
- ☼ Go on a walk outdoors with the students. Have them use your directions and map to guide the walk.

Student Diary Assignment
- ☐ With the students, fill out the nature journal sheet found on SD pg. 81. The students should sketch a map of your walk complete with a compass rose and a few natural landmarks.

Read-Alouds

Optional Encyclopedia Pages
- 📖 *The Usborne Children's Encyclopedia* - There are no new pages scheduled.

Optional Library Books
- 📖 *You Can Use a Compass* (Rookie Read-About Science) by Lisa Trumbauer
- 📖 *North, South, East, and West* (Rookie Read-About Science) by Allan Fowler
- 📖 *Maps and Globes* by Jack Knowlton and Harriet Barton

Coordinating Activities

These following activities will help you to reinforce the week's topic and main idea.

✂ **Art** – (Room Map) Have the students choose a room in your house. Use a compass to find where north, south, east, and west are in the room. Next, have the students draw the compass rose on a sheet of paper. Then, have them create a map showing the various items in the room.

Student Diary Assignment
- Have the students use SD pg. 80 to complete this activity.

Lapbook Assignment
- Have the students add the map to the "My Geology Projects" pocket in the lapbook.

- Snack – (Compass Cookies) Make your favorite sugar cookies, and then use icing to decorate them with the compass rose. Eat and enjoy.

Notes

Possible Schedules for Week 6

Two Days a Week Schedule	
Day 1	Day 2
❏ Read the introduction with the students. Color the main idea page. ❏ Complete the Hands-on Project "Head North, Child, North" and fill out the demonstration sheet.	❏ Complete the Hands-on Project: Nature Study "Nature Map" and fill out the nature journal sheet. ❏ Do the "Room Map" activity.
Supplies Needed for the Week ✓ Day 1: Compass, Map, Signs for north, south, east, and west, Chalk ✓ Day 2: Compass, Backyard map, Pencil, Paper	

Five Days a Week Schedule				
Day 1	Day 2	Day 3	Day 4	Day 5
❏ Read the introduction with the students. Color the main idea page. ❏ Eat "Compass Cookies" for snack.	❏ Complete the Hands-on Project "Head North, Child, North" and fill out the demonstration sheet. ❏ Choose one of the books from the read-aloud suggestions and read it to the students.	❏ Complete the Compass Mini-book. ❏ Choose one of the books from the read-aloud suggestions and read it to the students.	❏ Do the "Room Map" activity. ❏ Choose one of the books from the read-aloud suggestions and read it to the students.	❏ Complete the Hands-on Project: Nature Study "Nature Map" and fill out the nature journal sheet.
Supplies Needed for the Week ✓ Day 1: Compass, Map, Sugar cookies, Icing ✓ Day 2: Compass, Signs for north, south, east, and west, Chalk ✓ Day 4: Pencil, Paper ✓ Day 5: Compass, Backyard map				

Intro to Science
Unit 4: Intro to Meteorology

Intro to Meteorology Unit Overview

Sequence for Study
- Week 1: The Sun
- Week 2: The Water Cycle
- Week 3: The Seasons
- Week 4: Wind
- Week 5: Tornadoes
- Week 6: Thermometer

Supplies Needed for the Unit

Week	Introduction Props	Hands-on Project Materials	Coordinating Activities Supplies
1	*No supplies needed.*	Marshmallows, Chocolate squares, Muffin tin, Foil, Paper cup	Orange, SunPrint paper, Several squares of red, yellow, and orange tissue paper, Paper
2	Water Cycle Picture from pg. 188 of the Appendix	Jar with lid, Glass, Cold water, Towel, Ice	Egg whites, Cream of Tartar, Vanilla, Sugar, Jar, Ice, Salt, Water, Funnel, Spatula, Measuring cup, Small spray bottle or eyedropper, Blue paint, Paper
3	*No supplies needed.*	Cup, Food coloring (red and blue), Cold water, Salt, Ice on the ground	Paper, Seasonal pictures from magazines
4	*No supplies needed.*	Fan, File folder, Small, light objects	Blue Jell-O, Cool Whip, Container of bubbles, Paper
5	Pictures of tornadoes	2 2-L Plastic bottles, Knife, Plastic film canister, Food coloring	Frozen fruit, Ice cream, Milk or juice, Thick paintbrush, Paper, Black and white paint, Plate
6	Thermometer	Thermometer	Variety of hot and cold foods, Pictures of things to do or wear when it is hot, Pictures of things to do or wear when it is cold

Books Scheduled

Hands-on Projects (Required Books)
- *More Mudpies to Magnets (If you are using the scientific demonstration option.)*
- *Handbook of Nature Study (If you are using the nature study option.)*

Read-Aloud Suggestions

Optional Encyclopedia
- *The Usborne Children's Encyclopedia*

Week 1
- *The Sun: Our Nearest Star* (Let's-Read-and-Find Out) by Franklyn M. Branley and Edward Miller
- *Wake Up, Sun!* (Step-Into-Reading, Step 1) by David L. Harrison
- *The Sun Is My Favorite Star* by Frank Asch

Week 2
- *The Water Cycle* (First Facts, Water All Around) by Rebecca Olien
- *The Magic School Bus Wet All Over: A Book About The Water Cycle* by Pat Relf and Carolyn Bracken

Week 3
- *Watching the Seasons* (Welcome Books) by Edana Eckart
- *Sunshine Makes the Seasons* (Let's-Read-and-Find... Science 2) by Franklyn M. Branley and Michael Rex
- *Our Seasons* by Ranida T. Mckneally and Grace Lin

Week 4
- *Feel the Wind* (Let's-Read-and-Find... Science 2) by Arthur Dorros
- *The Wind Blew* by Pat Hutchins
- *Can You See the Wind?* (Rookie Read-About Science) by Allan Fowler

Week 5
- *Tornado Alert* (Let's-Read-and-Find... Science 2) by Franklyn M. Branley and Giulio Maestro
- *Tornadoes!* (DK READERS) by DK Publishing
- *The Terrifying Tub Tornado* by Ann K. Larson

Week 6
- *What Is a Thermometer* (Rookie Read-About Science) by Lisa Trumbauer
- *Thermometers* (First Facts. Science Tools) by Adele Richardson
- *Temperature* (Blastoff! Readers, First Science) by Kay Manolis
- *Too, Too Hot* (Reader's Clubhouse Level 1 Reader) by Judy Kentor Schmauss

The Sun ~ Week 1

Weekly Topic

Main Idea
- The energy from the sun heats our earth.

Introduction

If possible, share this introduction while you are outside on a sunny day. Begin by asking to the students:

> **?** *"When we look up in the sky during the day, what do we see?*

Give the students time to answer and point out the sun if they do not. (*Caution – DO NOT* look directly at the sun as it can damage your eyes.)

> *That's right! The sun plays a very important role for our earth. It gives us light during the day and provides just the right amount of heat for our planet.*

> *The energy created by lots of explosions on the sun heats up our earth. We can also capture this solar energy and use it for power!*

> *This week, we are going to look closer at the sun.*

Student Diary Assignment
- Have the students color the coloring page found on SD pg. 84.

Lapbook Assignment
- Have the students cut out and color the Sun Mini-book on LT pg. 37. You can have them cut out the main idea graphic included and glue it in the interior of the mini-book or you can write a sentence with what they have learned from the week for them on the inside of the mini-book. Once the students are done, have them glue the booklet into the mini-lapbook.

Hands-on Projects

Scientific Demonstration: Solar Warmer

In this demonstration, you will help the students to see how see how that the sun heats things up.

Materials Needed
- ✓ Marshmallows
- ✓ Chocolate squares
- ✓ Muffin tin
- ✓ Foil
- ✓ Paper cup

Steps to Complete
1. Follow the directions found on *More Mudpies to Magnets* pg. 107.

Student Diary Assignment
- ☐ With the students, fill out the demonstration sheet found on SD pg. 85.

Nature Study: Sunny Observations

This week, you are going to observe the effects of the sun. (*Caution – DO NOT look directly at the sun as it can damage your eyes.*)

Preparation
- Read the pp. 834-838 in the *Handbook of Nature Study* to learn more about the Sun.

Outdoor Time
- Go on a walk with the students to observe the effects of the sun. Stand in the shade and then stand in the full sun. Observe how different it feels. You can use the information you have learned from reading the *Handbook of Nature Study* to answer the their questions or to share information about what they are observing.

Student Diary Assignment
- ☐ With the students, fill out the nature journal sheet found on SD pg. 87. The students can sketch what they have seen or you can write down their observations.

Read-Alouds

Optional Encyclopedia Pages
- *The Usborne Children's Encyclopedia* pp. 262-263 (The Sun)

Optional Library Books
- *The Sun: Our Nearest Star* (Let's-Read-and-Find Out) by Franklyn M. Branley and Edward Miller

- *Wake Up, Sun!* (Step-Into-Reading, Step 1) by David L. Harrison
- *The Sun Is My Favorite Star* by Frank Asch

Coordinating Activities

These following activities will help you to reinforce the week's topic and main idea.

- **Art** – (Tissue Paper Sun) Give the students several squares of red, yellow, and orange tissue paper and a piece of paper with the outline of the sun. Have them glue the tissue paper sheets on the sun outline, overlapping them to create their own sun design. (*Note – You could also cut the tissue paper in circles instead if you want to emphasize the shape of a circle.*)

  Student Diary Assignment
  - Have the students use SD pg. 86 to complete this activity.

  Lapbook Assignment
  - Have the students cut out the "My Meteorology Projects" pocket on LT pg. 43. Have them glue the pocket into the lapbook and add their tissue paper sun to the pocket.

- **Snack** – (Sun Slices) Peel and slice an orange horizontally to form circles. Tell the students they are slices of the sun. Eat and enjoy!

- **More Fun** – (Sun Pictures) SunPrint paper is blue paper that turns white when exposed to the sun. It can be purchased at your local craft store or online. When you cover a portion of the SunPrint paper that part will remain blue while the part exposed to the sun turns white, creating a picture. Have the students lay out their design on the paper according to the directions that come with the paper. Then, lay the paper out in the sun and watch their creation develop.

Notes

Possible Schedules for Week 1

Two Days a Week Schedule	
Day 1	Day 2
❑ Read the introduction with the students. Color the main idea page. ❑ Complete the Hands-on Project "Solar Warmer" and fill out the demonstration sheet.	❑ Complete the Hands-on Project: Nature Study "Sunny Observations" and fill out the nature journal sheet. ❑ Do the "Tissue Paper Sun" activity.
Supplies Needed for the Week ✓ Day 1: Marshmallows, Chocolate squares, Muffin tin, Foil, Paper cup ✓ Day 2: Several squares of red, yellow, and orange tissue paper, Paper	

Five Days a Week Schedule				
Day 1	Day 2	Day 3	Day 4	Day 5
❑ Read the introduction with the students. Color the main idea page. ❑ Eat "Sun Slices" for snack.	❑ Complete the Hands-on Project "Solar Warmer" and fill out the demonstration sheet. ❑ Read the selected pages in *The Usborne Children's Encyclopedia*.	❑ Have some more fun with the "Sun Pictures" activity. ❑ Complete the The Sun Mini-book. ❑ Choose one of the books from the read-aloud suggestions and read it to the students.	❑ Do the "Tissue Paper Sun" activity. ❑ Choose one of the books from the read-aloud suggestions and read it to the students.	❑ Complete the Hands-on Project: Nature Study "Sunny Observations" and fill out the nature journal sheet.
Supplies Needed for the Week ✓ Day 1: Orange ✓ Day 2: Marshmallows, Chocolate squares, Muffin tin, Foil, Paper cup ✓ Day 3: SunPrint paper ✓ Day 4: Several squares of red, yellow, and orange tissue paper, Paper				

The Water Cycle ~ Week 2

Weekly Topic

Main Idea
- The water cycle shows the movement of water on the earth.

Introduction

Have a picture of the water cycle on the table in front of you. You can find a template of the water cycle on Appendix pg. 188. Say to the students:

The amount of water on the earth never changes. It just switches forms above and below the earth. We show the movement of water on the earth with something called the water cycle.

Point to the picture of the water cycle. (*Note – As you go through the next five steps, point to the place the step is shown on the water cycle sheet.*) Say to the students:

The water cycle begins with water in the oceans and the seas. The sun heats up the water in the seas, lakes, and oceans around the earth.

Next, invisible drops of water called water vapor, rise up into the air.

Then, these water vapor drops combine together and form clouds.

When the drops in the clouds get very heavy they fall to the ground as rain or snow.

This water runs back into rivers, lakes, and oceans to be heated up by the Sun again! This week, we are going to learn more about water vapor and the water cycle.

Student Diary Assignment
- Have the students color the coloring page found on SD pg. 88.

Lapbook Assignment
- Have the students cut out and color the Water Cycle Mini-book on LT pg. 38. You can have them cut out the main idea graphic included and glue it in the interior of the mini-book or you can write a sentence with what they have learned from the week for them on the inside of the mini-book. Once the students are done, have them glue the booklet into the mini-lapbook.

Hands-on Projects

Scientific Demonstration: Let's dew it

In this demonstration, you will help the students to see what water vapor is.

Materials Needed
- ✓ Jar with lid
- ✓ Glass
- ✓ Cold water
- ✓ Towel
- ✓ Ice

Steps to Complete
1. Follow the directions found on *More Mudpies to Magnets* pg. 108.

Student Diary Assignment
- With the students, fill out the demonstration sheet found on SD pg. 89.

Nature Study: Dewy Observations

This week, you are going to observe water vapor in the form of dew. (If you are lucky enough to have a rain storm this week, have the students observe the clouds and the ground before and after the storm.)

Preparation
- Read the pp. 808-814 in the *Handbook of Nature Study* to learn more about the various forms of water in nature.

Outdoor Time
- Go on a walk with the students early in the morning to observe the dew on the ground. Allow the students to make observations about what they find. You can use the information you have learned from reading the *Handbook of Nature Study* to answer their questions or to share information about what they are observing.

Student Diary Assignment
- With the students, fill out the nature journal sheet found on SD pg. 91. The students can sketch what they have seen or you can write down their observations.

Read-Alouds

Optional Encyclopedia Pages
- *The Usborne Children's Encyclopedia* pg. 14 (The Weather)

Optional Library Books

- *The Water Cycle* (First Facts, Water All Around) by Rebecca Olien
- *The Magic School Bus Wet All Over: A Book About The Water Cycle* by Pat Relf and Carolyn Bracken

Coordinating Activities

These following activities will help you to reinforce the week's topic and main idea.

- **Art** – (Raindrop Painting) Give the students a small spray bottle or eyedropper with blue paint that has been diluted with water. Have them rain down the paint (i.e., squirt) onto a sheet of paper.

    Student Diary Assignment
    - Have the students use SD pg. 90 to complete this activity.

    Lapbook Assignment
    - Have the students add the page they painted to the "My Meteorology Projects" pocket in the lapbook.

- **Snack** – (Clouds) Make a few clouds for the students to eat. Beat 2 egg whites with ¼ tsp of cream of tartar until stiff peaks form. Add in ½ tsp vanilla and ⅓ cup sugar. Beat until well incorporated. Drop spoonfuls on a cookie sheet lined with foil. Bake at 325°F for 10 min, then turn off the oven. (*Note – Don't open the oven door.*) Let the clouds sit in the oven for 50 more minutes. Remove and serve.

- **More Fun** – (You Can Dew It) Do another activity from *More Mudpies to Magnets*, "You Can Dew It" on pg. 115, with the students. This demonstration will help the students to learn more about water vapor. You will need a jar, ice, salt, water, a funnel, a spatula, and a measuring cup for this activity.

Notes

Possible Schedules for Week 2

Two Days a Week Schedule	
Day 1	Day 2
❑ Read the introduction with the students. Color the main idea page. ❑ Complete the Hands-on Project "Let's Dew It" and fill out the demonstration sheet.	❑ Complete the Hands-on Project: Nature Study "Dewy Observations" and fill out the nature journal sheet. ❑ Do the "Raindrop Painting" activity.
Supplies Needed for the Week ✓ Day 1: Water Cycle Picture, Jar with lid, Glass, Cold water, Towel, Ice ✓ Day 2: Small spray bottle or eyedropper, Blue paint, Paper	

Five Days a Week Schedule				
Day 1	Day 2	Day 3	Day 4	Day 5
❑ Read the introduction with the students. Color the main idea page. ❑ Eat "Clouds" for snack.	❑ Complete the Hands-on Project "Let's Dew It" and fill out the demonstration sheet. ❑ Read the selected pages in *The Usborne Children's Encyclopedia*.	❑ Have some more fun with the "You Can Dew It" activity. ❑ Complete the Water Cycle Mini-book. ❑ Choose one of the books from the read-aloud suggestions and read it to the students.	❑ Do the "Raindrop Painting" activity. ❑ Choose one of the books from the read-aloud suggestions and read it to the students.	❑ Complete the Hands-on Project: Nature Study "Dewy Observations" and fill out the nature journal sheet.
Supplies Needed for the Week ✓ Day 1: Water Cycle Picture, Egg whites, Cream of Tartar, Vanilla, Sugar ✓ Day 2: Jar with lid, Glass, Cold water, Towel, Ice ✓ Day 3: Jar, Ice, Salt, Water, Funnel, Spatula, Measuring cup ✓ Day 4: Small spray bottle or eyedropper, Blue paint, Paper				

The Seasons ~ Week 3

Weekly Topic

Main Idea
- Spring, summer, fall, and winter are all seasons.

Introduction
Say to the students:

A season is a collection of days with a typical weather pattern. On earth, we have four seasons – spring, summer, fall, and winter.

Typically, winter has shorter days of winter that can be filled with cold and snow. Around spring it warms and the flowers begin to bloom. During summer, the days are longer and hotter. And finally, fall is marked by a drop in the temperature and a change in the leaves.

? *Can you guess what season it is now?*

Allow the students to answer and provide them with the correct season if they do not guess it. Then, say to the students:

Winter, spring, summer, and fall are all seasons. This week, we are going to learn more about the seasons.

Student Diary Assignment
- Have the students color the coloring page found on SD pg. 92.

Lapbook Assignment
- Have the students cut out and color the Seasons Mini-book on LT pg. 39. You can have them cut out the main idea graphic included and glue it in the interior of the mini-book or you can write a sentence with what they have learned from the week for them on the inside of the mini-book. Once the students are done, have them glue the booklet into the mini-lapbook.

Hands-on Projects

Scientific Demonstration: The Big Meltdown

In this demonstration, you will help the students to see how salt helps to melt ice in the winter.

Materials Needed
- ✓ Cup
- ✓ Food coloring (red and blue)
- ✓ Cold water
- ✓ Salt
- ✓ Ice on the sidewalk or ground (If you don't have ice outside, freeze a pan of water the night before you do this activity.)

Steps to Complete
1. Follow the directions found on *More Mudpies to Magnets* pg. 111.

Student Diary Assignment
- With the students, fill out the demonstration sheet found on SD pg. 93.

Nature Study: Seasonal tree study

This week, you will begin a seasonal tree study.

Preparation
- Read the pp. 618-625 in the *Handbook of Nature Study* to learn more about trees and tree study.

Outdoor Time
- Go on a walk with the students to choose a tree they want to study in each season. Allow the students to make observations about what they find. You can use the information you have learned from reading the *Handbook of Nature Study* to answer their questions or to share information about what they are observing. When you get home, make an entry into their nature journal for the current season you are in. (*Note – Continue this tree study for the remaining three seasons over the year.*)

Student Diary Assignment
- With the students, fill out the nature journal sheet found on SD pg. 95. The students can sketch what they have seen or you can write down their observations. (*Note – When you do this project again in a few months you can use the same nature journal sheet.*)

Read-Alouds

Optional Encyclopedia Pages
- *The Usborne Children's Encyclopedia* pp. 12-13 (The Seasons)

Optional Library Books

- *Watching the Seasons* (Welcome Books) by Edana Eckart
- *Sunshine Makes the Seasons* (Let's-Read-and-Find... Science 2) by Franklyn M. Branley and Michael Rex
- *Our Seasons* by Ranida T. Mckneally and Grace Lin

Coordinating Activities

These following activities will help you to reinforce the week's topic and main idea.

✂ **Art** – (Seasons Collage) Make a collage for the season you are in using pictures from magazines. For example, if you do this week during the winter, use pictures of snowflakes, bare trees, icicles, Christmas trees and so on. Have the students glue the pictures on a sheet of paper as a collage.

Student Diary Assignment
- Have the students use SD pg. 94 to complete this activity.

Lapbook Assignment
- Have the students add their seasons collage to the "My Meteorology Projects" pocket in the lapbook.

✂ **More Fun** – (Seasons Book) Talk about the different things you see in each season. Then, have the students make a book with a page for each season. You can have them draw their own pictures or you can use stickers or magazine pictures to complete the project.

Notes

Possible Schedules for Week 3

Two Days a Week Schedule	
Day 1	Day 2
❑ Read the introduction with the students. Color the main idea page. ❑ Complete the Hands-on Project "The Big Meltdown" and fill out the demonstration sheet.	❑ Complete the Hands-on Project: Nature Study "Seasonal Tree Study" and fill out the nature journal sheet. ❑ Do the "Seasons Collage" activity.
Supplies Needed for the Week ✓ Day 1: Cup, Food coloring (red and blue), Cold water, Salt, Ice on the ground ✓ Day 2: Seasonal pictures from magazines	

Five Days a Week Schedule				
Day 1	Day 2	Day 3	Day 4	Day 5
❑ Read the introduction with the students. Color the main idea page. ❑ Choose one of the books from the read-aloud suggestions and read it to the students.	❑ Complete the Hands-on Project "The Big Meltdown" and fill out the demonstration sheet. ❑ Read the selected pages in *The Usborne Children's Encyclopedia*.	❑ Have some more fun with the "Seasons Book" activity. ❑ Complete the Seasons Mini-book.	❑ Do the "Seasons Collage" activity. ❑ Choose one of the books from the read-aloud suggestions and read it to the students.	❑ Complete the Hands-on Project: Nature Study "Seasonal Tree Study" and fill out the nature journal sheet.
Supplies Needed for the Week ✓ Day 2: Cup, Food coloring (red and blue), Cold water, Salt, Ice on the ground ✓ Day 3: Paper ✓ Day 4: Seasonal pictures from magazines				

Wind ~ Week 4

Weekly Topic

Main Idea
- When air moves it causes wind.

Introduction
If possible, share this introduction while you are outside on a windy day. Say to the students:

When air moves, it causes what we know as wind.

> **?** *Can you think of a sign of a windy day?*

Let the students share a few ideas and then say to the students:

Those are good ideas. When it's windy out, we can see the grass and leaves blow. The tree branches bend and sway.

Wind is caused by the uneven heating of the surface of the Earth. As the sun heats up the surface and the air around it, the warm air rises. This uneven heating causes air to move around, creating wind.

This week, we are going to spend some time learning about the wind.

Student Diary Assignment
- Have the students color the coloring page found on SD pg. 96.

Lapbook Assignment
- Have the students cut out and color the Wind Mini-book on LT pg. 40. You can have them cut out the main idea graphic included and glue it in the interior of the mini-book or you can write a sentence with what they have learned from the week for them on the inside of the mini-book. Once the students are done, have them glue the booklet into the mini-lapbook.

Hands-on Projects

Scientific Demonstration: Blow Wind Blow
In this demonstration, you will help the students to test wind power and speed.

Materials Needed
- ✓ Fan
- ✓ File folder
- ✓ Small, light objects (i.e., small pieces of paper, feathers, pieces of Styrofoam cups, small rubber balls, leaves)

Steps to Complete
1. Follow the directions found on *More Mudpies to Magnets* pg. 112.

Student Diary Assignment
- ☐ With the students, fill out the demonstration sheet found on SD pg. 97.

Nature Study: Wind

This week, you will observe the wind. (*Note – If you do not have a breezy day, wait until you do have one to do this nature study.*)

Preparation
- ↻ Read the pp. 791-798 in the *Handbook of Nature Study* to learn more about the winds of the world.

Outdoor Time
- ☼ Go on a walk with the students to observe the signs of wind. Allow the students to make observations about what they find. You can use the information you have learned from reading the *Handbook of Nature Study* to answer their questions or to share information about what they are observing.

Student Diary Assignment
- ☐ With the students, fill out the nature journal sheet found on SD pg. 99. The students can sketch what they have seen or you can write down their observations.

Read-Alouds

Optional Encyclopedia Pages
- 📖 *The Usborne Children's Encyclopedia* pg. 15 (Windy Weather)

Optional Library Books
- 📖 *Feel the Wind* (Let's-Read-and-Find... Science 2) by Arthur Dorros
- 📖 *The Wind Blew* by Pat Hutchins
- 📖 *Can You See the Wind?* (Rookie Read-About Science) by Allan Fowler

Coordinating Activities

These following activities will help you to reinforce the week's topic and main idea.

✂ **Art** – (Draw a Storm) Have the students draw a picture of a storm on a piece of paper. Let their imaginations run free for this project!

Student Diary Assignment
 ☐ Have the students use SD pg. 98 to complete this activity.

Lapbook Assignment
 📁 Have the students add their collage to the "My Meteorology Projects" pocket in the lapbook.

✂ **Snack** – (Jell-O Storms) Make your favorite blue-colored Jell-O and fill a clear cup halfway with it for the rain. Then, top the rain Jell-O off with Cool Whip for clouds! (*Note – You could use food coloring to tint the cool whip gray for more authentic rain clouds.*)

✂ **More Fun** – (Hot Bubble Flier) Do another activity from *More Mudpies to Magnets*, "Hot Bubble Flier" on pg. 106, with the students. This demonstration will help see what happens to warm bubbles on a cold day. You will need a container of bubbles for this activity.

Notes

Possible Schedules for Week 4

Two Days a Week Schedule	
Day 1	Day 2
❑ Read the introduction with the students. Color the main idea page. ❑ Complete the Hands-on Project "Blow Wind Blow" and fill out the demonstration sheet.	❑ Complete the Hands-on Project: Nature Study "Wind" and fill out the nature journal sheet. ❑ Do the "Draw a Storm" activity.
Supplies Needed for the Week ✓ Day 1: Fan, File folder, Small, light objects (i.e., small pieces of paper, feathers, pieces of Styrofoam cups, small rubber balls, leaves) ✓ Day 2: Paper	

Five Days a Week Schedule				
Day 1	Day 2	Day 3	Day 4	Day 5
❑ Read the introduction with the students. Color the main idea page. ❑ Eat "Jell-O Storms" for snack.	❑ Complete the Hands-on Project "Blow Wind Blow" and fill out the demonstration sheet. ❑ Read the selected pages in *The Usborne Children's Encyclopedia*.	❑ Have some more fun with the "Hot Bubble Fliers" activity. ❑ Complete the Wind Mini-book. ❑ Choose one of the books from the read-aloud suggestions and read it to the students.	❑ Do the "Draw a Storm" activity. ❑ Choose one of the books from the read-aloud suggestions and read it to the students.	❑ Complete the Hands-on Project: Nature Study "Wind" and fill out the nature journal sheet.
Supplies Needed for the Week ✓ Day 1: Blue Jell-O, Cool Whip ✓ Day 2: Fan, File folder, Small, light objects (i.e., small pieces of paper, feathers, pieces of Styrofoam cups, small rubber balls, leaves) ✓ Day 3: Container of bubbles ✓ Day 4: Paper				

Tornadoes ~ Week 5

Weekly Topic

Main Idea
- Tornadoes are funnels of spinning wind.

Introduction

Have pictures of tornadoes, either from magazines or off the Internet, on the table in front of you. Say to the students:

These are all pictures of tornadoes. Tornadoes are funnels of spinning wind that touch the ground and are connected to the clouds above.

Most tornadoes only last a few minutes, but in that time they can tear up trees and houses, plus move cars, animals, and people.

They typically form in the spring in the middle of a very strong storm.

This week, we are going to learn more about tornadoes.

If you live in a tornado prone area, this would be a good week to learn more about tornado safety.

Student Diary Assignment
- Have the students color the coloring page found on SD pg. 100.

Lapbook Assignment
- Have the students cut out and color the Tornado Mini-book on LT pg. 41. You can have them cut out the main idea graphic included and glue it in the interior of the mini-book or you can write a sentence with what they have learned from the week for them on the inside of the mini-book. Once the students are done, have them glue the booklet into the mini-lapbook.

Hands-on Projects

Scientific Demonstration: Tornado Tower

In this demonstration, you will help the students to see how a tornado works.

Materials Needed
- ✓ 2 2-L Plastic bottles

- ✓ Knife
- ✓ Plastic film canister
- ✓ Food coloring

Steps to Complete
1. Follow the directions found on *More Mudpies to Magnets* pg. 114.

Student Diary Assignment
- ☐ With the students, fill out the demonstration sheet found on SD pg. 101.

Nature Study: Tornadoes

This week, you won't be heading outside to observe tornadoes as that would be too dangerous! Instead, you will be looking at a website about tornadoes and then creating a journal page with what the students have learned. If you do have a thunderstorm this week, take a moment to observe it from the inside of your home.

Preparation
- Look over the website below to determine what parts of it you want to highlight.

Outdoor Time
- Spend some time on this website to learn more about tornadoes.
- http://www.weatherwizkids.com/weather-tornado.htm

Student Diary Assignment
- ☐ With the students, fill out the nature journal sheet found on SD pg. 103. The students can sketch what they have seen or you can write down their observations.

Read-Alouds

Optional Encyclopedia Pages
- *The Usborne Children's Encyclopedia* pp. 16-17 Storms and flood

Optional Library Books
- *Tornado Alert* (Let's-Read-and-Find... Science 2) by Franklyn M. Branley and Giulio Maestro
- *Tornadoes!* (DK READERS) by DK Publishing
- *The Terrifying Tub Tornado* by Ann K. Larson

Coordinating Activities

These following activities will help you to reinforce the week's topic and main idea.

✂ **Art** – (Swirling Art) Give the students a thick paintbrush, a piece of paper, and some black and white paint on a plate. Have them get a bit of black and white paint on the paintbrush and make swirls on the paper until they have created a gray-swirly tornado.

Student Diary Assignment
- Have the students use SD pg. 102 to complete this activity.

Lapbook Assignment
- Have the students add their painting to the "My Meteorology Projects" pocket in the lapbook.

✂ **Snack** – (Tornado Smoothies) Blend ½ cup of your favorite frozen fruit (strawberries or peaches), ½ cup of ice cream, and ½ cup milk or juice. First, blend the fruit and milk together until well blended, then add the ice cream and whip until smooth.

Notes

Possible Schedules for Week 5

Two Days a Week Schedule	
Day 1	Day 2
❏ Read the introduction with the students. Color the main idea page. ❏ Complete the Hands-on Project "Tornado Tower" and fill out the demonstration sheet.	❏ Complete the Hands-on Project: Nature Study "Tornadoes" and fill out the nature journal sheet. ❏ Do the "Swirling Art" activity.
Supplies Needed for the Week ✓ Day 1: Pictures of tornadoes, 2 2-L Plastic bottles, Knife, Plastic film canister, Food coloring ✓ Day 2: Thick paintbrush, Paper, Black and white paint, Plate	

Five Days a Week Schedule				
Day 1	Day 2	Day 3	Day 4	Day 5
❏ Read the introduction with the students. Color the main idea page. ❏ Eat "Tornado Smoothies" for snack.	❏ Complete the Hands-on Project "Tornado Tower" and fill out the demonstration sheet. ❏ Read the selected pages in *The Usborne Children's Encyclopedia*.	❏ Complete the Tornadoes Mini-book. ❏ Choose one of the books from the read-aloud suggestions and read it to the students.	❏ Do the "Swirling Art" activity. ❏ Choose one of the books from the read-aloud suggestions and read it to the students.	❏ Complete the Hands-on Project: Nature Study "Tornadoes" and fill out the nature journal sheet.
Supplies Needed for the Week ✓ Day 1: Pictures of tornadoes, Frozen fruit, Ice cream, Milk or juice ✓ Day 2: 2 2-L Plastic bottles, Knife, Plastic film canister, Food coloring ✓ Day 4: Thick paintbrush, Paper, Black and white paint, Plate				

Thermometer ~ Week 6

Weekly Topic

Main Idea
- A thermometer tells us whether it is hot or cold.

Introduction
Have a thermometer on the table in front of you. Say to the students:

This is a thermometer. Its job is to tell us whether it is hot or cold.

Demonstrate to the students how to read a thermometer. Then place your finger over the bulb at the bottom of the thermometer to heat it up.

? *Can you see how the line rises when I heat it up with my thumb?*

The higher the line on a thermometer is, the hotter it is. The lower the line on the thermometer is, the colder it is.

This week, we are going to learn more about thermometers.

Student Diary Assignment
- Have the students color the coloring page found on SD pg. 104.

Lapbook Assignment
- Have the students cut out and color the Thermometer Mini-book on LT pg. 42. You can have them cut out the main idea graphic included and glue it in the interior of the mini-book or you can write a sentence with what they have learned from the week for them on the inside of the mini-book. Once the students are done, have them glue the booklet into the mini-lapbook.

Hands-on Projects

Scientific Demonstration: Hot and Cold – Let's Get Precise

In this demonstration, you will help the students to learn more about temperature.

Materials Needed
- ✓ Thermometer

Steps to Complete
1. Follow the directions found on *More Mudpies to Magnets* pg. 113.

Student Diary Assignment
- With the students, fill out the demonstration sheet found on SD pg. 105.

Nature Study: Temperature and Thermometers

This week, you will be examining outdoor temperatures.

Preparation
- Read the pp. 790-791 in the *Handbook of Nature Study* to learn more about temperature and thermometers.

Outdoor Time
- Go on a walk with the students to observe the temperature and how it makes you feel. Be sure to find a thermometer (or bring your own) to observe while on your walk. You can use the information you have learned from reading the *Handbook of Nature Study* to answer their questions or to share information about what they are observing.

Student Diary Assignment
- With the students, fill out the nature journal sheet found on SD pg. 107. The students can sketch what they have seen or you can write down their observations.

Read-Alouds

Optional Encyclopedia Pages
- *The Usborne Children's Encyclopedia* pp. 196-197 (Hot and Cold)

Optional Library Books
- *What Is a Thermometer* (Rookie Read-About Science) by Lisa Trumbauer
- *Thermometers* (First Facts. Science Tools) by Adele Richardson
- *Temperature* (Blastoff! Readers, First Science) by Kay Manolis
- *Too, Too Hot* (Reader's Clubhouse Level 1 Reader) by Judy Kentor Schmauss

Coordinating Activities

These following activities will help you to reinforce the week's topic and main idea.

- **Art** – (Temperature Collage) Have the students cut out magazine pictures or use stickers to make their collage. On one half of a sheet of paper or poster board, have them paste pictures of things you do or use when it is hot. On the other half, have them paste pictures of things you do or use when it is cold.

Student Diary Assignment
☐ Have the students use SD pg. 106 to complete this activity.

Lapbook Assignment
📁 Have the students add their collage to the "My Meteorology Projects" pocket in the lapbook.

✂ Snack – (Hot and Cold) Choose two or three warm foods, such as tea or soup, and two or three cold foods, such as cheese or ice cream. Have the students use a food thermometer (not a mercury thermometer) to test the temperature of each food. Then eat the food as you talk about the differences.

Notes

Possible Schedules for Week 6

Two Days a Week Schedule	
Day 1	Day 2
❏ Read the introduction with the students. Color the main idea page. ❏ Complete the Hands-on Project "Hot and Cold: Let's Get Precise" and fill out the demonstration sheet.	❏ Complete the Hands-on Project: Nature Study "Temperature and Thermometers" and fill out the nature journal sheet. ❏ Do the "Temperature Collage" activity.
Supplies Needed for the Week ✓ Day 1: Thermometer ✓ Day 2: Thermometer, Pictures of things to do or wear when it is hot, Pictures of things to do or wear when it is cold	

Five Days a Week Schedule				
Day 1	Day 2	Day 3	Day 4	Day 5
❏ Read the introduction with the students. Color the main idea page. ❏ Eat "Hot and Cold" for snack.	❏ Complete the Hands-on Project "Hot and Cold: Let's Get Precise" and fill out the demonstration sheet. ❏ Read the selected pages in *The Usborne Children's Encyclopedia*.	❏ Complete the Thermometer Mini-book. ❏ Choose one of the books from the read-aloud suggestions and read it to the students.	❏ Do the "Temperature Collage" activity. ❏ Choose one of the books from the read-aloud suggestions and read it to the students.	❏ Complete the Hands-on Project: Nature Study "Temperature and Thermometers" and fill out the nature journal sheet.
Supplies Needed for the Week ✓ Day 1: Thermometer, Variety of hot and cold foods ✓ Day 2: Thermometer ✓ Day 4: Pictures of things to do or wear when it is hot, Pictures of things to do or wear when it is cold ✓ Day 5: Thermometer				

Intro to Science
Unit 5: Intro to Botany

Intro to Botany Unit Overview

Sequence for Study
- Week 1: Plants
- Week 2: Flowers
- Week 3: Seeds
- Week 4: Leaves
- Week 5: Stems
- Week 6: Roots

Supplies Needed for the Unit

Week	Introduction Props	Hands-on Project Materials	Coordinating Activities Supplies
1	Small potted plant	Shoe box, Dividers to place in the box, Scissors, 1 Small potted plant, preferably a vine plant such as ivy, Water	Potato or carrot sticks, Celery, Lettuce, Berries, Small pot, Dirt, Bean seed, Tissue paper squares (brown, green, red, and purple), Glue, Paper
2	Plant with a flower	Tulip, Razor or knife, Magnifying glass, Q-tip	Cake with icing flowers, Borax, Corn meal, Jar, Wildflowers, Paint, Paper
3	Lima bean seed (soaked overnight)	Bean seeds, Ziploc baggy, Paper towel, Water, Collected seeds, Eggshell	Several different fruits and seeds to eat, Red paint, Apple, Plate, Paper
4	Bean plant	Bean plant, Paper, Paper clip, Leaves, Paint	Edible leaves (lettuce, spinach, kale or bok choy), Ranch dressing, Sheet of cardboard, Leaves, Crayons, Paper
5	Celery, Magnifying glass	Celery (with leaves), Food coloring, Glass, Water	Celery Sticks, Cream Cheese, Brown and green paint, Straw, Water, Paper
6	Green onion with roots	Clear plastic cups, Cardboard, Sprouted plant, Cotton, Liquid plant food, Water	Green onion with roots, Carrot sticks or shoestring potato sticks, Green onion with roots, Paint, Paper

Books Scheduled

Hands-on Projects (Required Books)
- *More Mudpies to Magnets* (If you are using the scientific demonstration option.)
- *Handbook of Nature Study* (If you are using the nature study option.)

Read-Aloud Suggestions

Optional Encyclopedia
- *The Usborne Children's Encyclopedia*

Week 1
- *From Seed to Plant* (Rookie Read-About Science) by Allan Fowler
- *From Seed to Plant* by Gail Gibbons

Week 2
- *The Reason for a Flower* (Ruth Heller's World of Nature) by Ruth Heller
- *Planting a Rainbow* by Lois Ehler

Week 3
- *The Magic School Bus Plants Seeds: A Book About How Living Things Grow* by Joanna Cole
- *Seeds* by Ken Robbins
- *A Fruit Is a Suitcase for Seeds* by Jean Richards and Anca Hariton
- *Curious George Plants a Seed* (Curious George Early Readers) by H. A. Rey

Week 4
- *Leaves* (Plant Parts series) (Pebble Plus: Plant Parts) by Vijaya Bodach,
- *I Am A Leaf* (Level 1 - Hello Reader) by Jean Marzollo and Judith Moffatt
- *Leaves* by David Ezra Stein

Week 5
- *Stems* (Plant Parts) by Vijaya Bodach
- *Plant Stems & Roots* (Look Once, Look Again Science Series) by David M. Schwartz
- *Stems* (First Step Nonfiction) by Melanie Mitchell

Week 6
- *Roots* (First Step Nonfiction) by Melanie Mitchell
- *Roots* (Plant Parts series) (Pebble Plus: Plant Parts) by Vijaya Bodach
- *Plant Plumbing: A Book About Roots and Stems* by Susan Blackaby

Plants ~ Week 1

Weekly Topic

Main Idea
- Plants grow toward the light.

Introduction
Have a small potted plant out on the table in front of you. Say to the students:

Let's take a look at this plant.

? *What do you notice about it?*

You can ask questions like what color is it, how does it feel, what does it smell like, if you student needs more guidance for their observations.

Those are great observations! Plants use light, water, and air to make food. We call the process they use to make food photosynthesis.

And since plants need light to make food, they will typically grow toward the light. Doing this makes it easier for them to get the sunlight they need to make food.

This week, we are going to look closer at plants.

Over the next several weeks, you will look at the different parts of a plant, but you may want to introduce them now (i.e., roots, stem, leaves, flowers, and fruit).

Student Diary Assignment
- Have the students color the coloring page found on SD pg. 110.

Lapbook Assignment
- Have the students cut out and color the Plants Mini-book on LT pg. 47. You can have them cut out the main idea graphic included and glue it in the interior of the mini-book or you can write a sentence with what they have learned from the week for them on the inside of the mini-book. Once the students are done, have them glue the booklet into the mini-lapbook.

Hands-on Projects

Scientific Demonstration: The Amazing Plant Maze

In this demonstration, you will help the students to see how far a plant will go to reach the light.

Materials Needed
- ✓ Shoe box
- ✓ Dividers to place in the box
- ✓ Scissors
- ✓ 1 Small potted plant, preferably a vine plant such as ivy
- ✓ Water
- ✓ Masking tape

Steps to Complete
1. Follow the directions found on *More Mudpies to Magnets* pg. 156.

Student Diary Assignment
- ☐ With the students, fill out the demonstration sheet found on SD pg. 111.

Nature Study: Plants

This week, you will begin to look at the plants found in the habitat in which you live.

Preparation
- Read the pp. 453-456 in the *Handbook of Nature Study* to learn more about plants and how to guide a study of plants in nature.

Outdoor Time
- Go on a walk and observe the different types of plants you see. If you can, take a walk in the woods to observe how plants tend to grow on the forest floor in places where more light gets through. Allow them to make additional observations while also guiding them to see that plants have leaves and stems.

Student Diary Assignment
- ☐ With the students, fill out the nature journal sheet found on SD pg. 113. The students can sketch what they have seen or you can write down their observations.

Read-Alouds

Optional Encyclopedia Pages
- *The Usborne Children's Encyclopedia* pg. 92 (Plant World)

Optional Library Books
- *From Seed to Plant* (Rookie Read-About Science) by Allan Fowler
- *From Seed to Plant* by Gail Gibbons

Coordinating Activities

These following activities will help you to reinforce the week's topic and main idea.

✂ **Art** – (Mosaic Plant) Cut up squares of different colors of tissue paper for the different plant parts, e.g., brown for the stem, green for the leaves, red for the fruit, and purple for the flowers. Have the students ball up the paper and glue it onto a black-line image or drawing of a plant. When they are finished, have them color the sun above the flower to remind them that plants grow toward the light.

Student Diary Assignment
- Have the students use SD pg. 112 to complete this activity.

Lapbook Assignment
- Have the students cut out the "My Botany Projects" pocket on LT pg. 53. Have them glue the pocket into the lapbook and add the project they just did to the pocket.

✂ **Snack** – (Edible Plants) Explain to the students that we eat many different types of plants and different parts of the plant - they are our vegetables and fruits! Then, let the students create a plant out of food. You can let them use potato or carrot sticks from the roots, celery for the stem, lettuce for the leaves, and berries for the fruit. Take a picture, then eat it all up!

✂ **More Fun** – (Bean Plant) Plant a seed in a pot, be sure to water it as needed and watch it grow! (*In week 4 of this unit, you will need a bean plant for the experiment, so you may want to do this activity this week to ensure that you have a bean plant for that week.*)

Notes

Possible Schedules for Week 1

Two Days a Week Schedule	
Day 1	Day 2
❑ Read the introduction with the students. Color the main idea page. ❑ Complete the Hands-on Project "The Amazing Plant Maze" and fill out the demonstration sheet.	❑ Complete the Hands-on Project: Nature Study "Plants" and fill out the nature journal sheet. ❑ Do the "Mosaic Plant" activity.
Supplies Needed for the Week ✓ Day 1: Shoe box, Dividers to place in the box, Scissors, 1 Small potted plant, preferably a vine plant such as ivy, Water ✓ Masking tape ✓ Day 2: Tissue paper squares (brown, green, red, and purple), Glue, Paper	

Five Days a Week Schedule				
Day 1	Day 2	Day 3	Day 4	Day 5
❑ Read the introduction with the students. Color the main idea page. ❑ Eat "Edible Plants" for snack.	❑ Complete the Hands-on Project "The Amazing Plant Maze" and fill out the demonstration sheet. ❑ Read the selected pages in *The Usborne Children's Encyclopedia*.	❑ Have some more fun with the "Bean Plant" demonstration. ❑ Complete the Plants Mini-book. ❑ Choose one of the books from the read-aloud suggestions and read it to the students.	❑ Do the "Mosaic Plant" activity. ❑ Choose one of the books from the read-aloud suggestions and read it to the students.	❑ Complete the Hands-on Project: Nature Study "Plants" and fill out the nature journal sheet.
Supplies Needed for the Week ✓ Day 1: Small potted plant, Potato or carrot sticks, Celery, Lettuce, Berries ✓ Day 2: Shoe box, Dividers to place in the box, Scissors, 1 Small potted plant, preferably a vine plant such as ivy, Water ✓ Day 3: Small pot, Dirt, Bean seed ✓ Day 4: Tissue paper squares (brown, green, red, and purple), Glue, Paper				

Flowers ~ Week 2

Weekly Topic

Main Idea
- Flowers have the parts of a plant needed to make a seed.

Introduction

Have a plant with a flower out on the table in front of you. Look for a plant that has a full flower with the parts visible and if possible a bud that has not opened yet. (*Note – If you can't find a plant like this, you can use the labeled sketch on pg. 189 of the Appendix.*) Say to the students:

This flower has all the parts of a plant that are needed to make a seed. After the flower is pollinated, it can produce a seed from which a baby plant can grow.

As you describe the different parts point to them on your plant or on the sheet from the Appendix.

All flowers begin as buds. The bud open up and develops into a flower with petals to help attract insects toward the center of the flower.

In the center of the flower are the parts of the plant, like the pistil and stamen, that are need to make the seed.

Insects or the wind move the pollen from the stamen to the top of the pistil of the flower. The pollen then travels down a tube in the pistil and a seed is formed. We call this process pollination and it's the main reason plants have flowers!

This week, we are going to look closer at flowers.

Student Diary Assignment
- Have the students color the coloring page found on SD pg. 114.

Lapbook Assignment
- Have the students cut out and color the Flowers Mini-book on LT pg. 48. You can have them cut out the main idea graphic included and glue it in the interior of the mini-book or you can write a sentence with what they have learned from the week for them on the inside of the mini-book. Once the students are done, have them glue the booklet into the mini-lapbook.

Hands-on Projects

Scientific Demonstration: Dissecting a Flower

In this demonstration, you will help the students will have a chance to observe all the parts of a flower.

Materials Needed
- ✓ Tulip (or other single flower with clearly defined parts)
- ✓ Razor or knife
- ✓ Magnifying glass
- ✓ Q-tip

Steps to Complete
1. Give each student a tulip bloom to examine. Use the diagram above to help point out the parts of the flower as they observe the bloom. Begin by pointing out the petals of the flower and explain that these are there to help attract insects to the flower.
2. Next, point out the anthers and the pollen on them. Share with the students that these are known as the male parts of a flower. Cut one of the anthers and use the magnifying glass to look at the pollen. (**Note**—*Be careful with the pollen as it can stain clothing*).
3. Then, point out the pistil in the center and share that this are the female parts of a flower. Use a q-tip to show how a pollinator transfers the pollen to the top of the pistil. Cut out the pistil and split it in half so that your students can observe the inside.
4. Allow your students time to make additional observations.

Student Diary Assignment
☐ With the students, fill out the demonstration sheet found on SD pg. 115.

Nature Study: Flowers

This week, you will look at the different flowers in your neighborhood.

Preparation
✎ Read the pp. 456-457 in the *Handbook of Nature Study* to learn more about flowers and their purpose.

Outdoor Time
✿ Go on a walk and observe the different types of flowers around the path. Allow the students to observe the flowers, look for the parts they know, and ask any questions they may have. You can use the information you have learned from

reading the *Handbook of Nature Study* to answer their questions or to share information about what they are observing.

Student Diary Assignment
☐ With the students, fill out the nature journal sheet found on SD pg. 117. The students can sketch what they have seen or you can write down their observations.

Read-Alouds

Optional Encyclopedia Pages
- *The Usborne Children's Encyclopedia* pg. 93 (Flowering Plants)

Optional Library Books
- *The Reason for a Flower* (Ruth Heller's World of Nature) by Ruth Heller
- *Planting a Rainbow* by Lois Ehler

Coordinating Activities

These following activities will help you to reinforce the week's topic and main idea.

✂ **Art** – (Field of Flowers) Have the students paint a field of flowers on a sheet of paper. Let the students' imaginations run free for this project, the results will be beautiful and interesting!

Student Diary Assignment
☐ Have the students use SD pg. 116 to complete this activity.

Lapbook Assignment
📁 Have the students add the page they painted to the "My Botany Projects" pocket in the lapbook.

✂ **Snack** – (Flower Cake) Have a piece of cake that is decorated with icing flowers.

✂ **More Fun** – (Flowers Forever) Do another activity from *More Mudpies to Magnets*, "Flowers Forever" on pg. 149, with the students. This demonstration will help the students to preserve a flower. You will need Borax, corn meal, a jar, and wildflowers for this activity.

Notes

Possible Schedules for Week 2

Two Days a Week Schedule	
Day 1	Day 2
❑ Read the introduction with the students. Color the main idea page. ❑ Complete the Hands-on Project "Dissecting a Flower" and fill out the demonstration sheet.	❑ Complete the Hands-on Project: Nature Study "Flowers" and fill out the nature journal sheet. ❑ Do the "Field of Flowers" activity.
Supplies Needed for the Week ✓ Day 1: Plant with a flower, Tulip, Razor or knife, Magnifying glass, Q-tip ✓ Day 2:	

Five Days a Week Schedule				
Day 1	Day 2	Day 3	Day 4	Day 5
❑ Read the introduction with the students. Color the main idea page. ❑ Eat "Cake Flowers" for snack.	❑ Complete the Hands-on Project "Dissecting a Flower" and fill out the demonstration sheet. ❑ Read the selected pages in *The Usborne Children's Encyclopedia*.	❑ Have some more fun with the "Flowers Forever" activity. ❑ Complete the Flowers Mini-book. ❑ Choose one of the books from the read-aloud suggestions and read it to the students.	❑ Do the "Field of Flowers" activity. ❑ Choose one of the books from the read-aloud suggestions and read it to the students.	❑ Complete the Hands-on Project: Nature Study "Flowers" and fill out the nature journal sheet.
Supplies Needed for the Week ✓ Day 1: Plant with a flower, Cake with icing flowers ✓ Day 2: Tulip, Razor or knife, Magnifying glass, Q-tip ✓ Day 3: Borax, Corn meal, Jar, Wildflowers ✓ Day 4: Paint, Paper				

Seeds ~ Week 3

Weekly Topic

Main Idea
- Seeds contain tiny baby plants.

Introduction

(Note – You will need to soak a bean seed overnight for this week's introduction.)

Have a lima bean seed that has been soaked overnight out on a plate on the table in front of you. Say to the students:

Last week we looked at flowers and how they have the parts of the plant that are needed to make a seed. This week, we are going to look closer at the seeds.

As you describe the different parts of the seed point to them on the lima bean or on the sheet from the Appendix on pg. 190.

A seed contains a baby plant in it. On the outside of the seed is the seed coat, which protects what is inside.

Most of what is inside the seed is a food store for the baby plant, but at the top, there is very beginning of the plant which starts at the radicle.

The little offshoot, called the epicotyl and hypocotyl develop into the roots and the stem with leaves when the conditions are right.

This week, we are going to take a closer look at seeds.

Student Diary Assignment
- Have the students color the coloring page found on SD pg. 118.

Lapbook Assignment
- Have the students cut out and color the Seeds Mini-book on LT pg. 49. You can have them cut out the main idea graphic included and glue it in the interior of the mini-book or you can write a sentence with what they have learned from the week for them on the inside of the mini-book. Once the students are done, have them glue the booklet into the mini-lapbook.

Hands-on Projects

Scientific Demonstration: Upside-down Plant

In this demonstration, the students to see what happens when seeds germinate.

Materials Needed
- ✓ Bean seeds
- ✓ Ziploc baggy
- ✓ Paper towel
- ✓ Water

Steps to Complete
1. Follow the directions found on *More Mudpies to Magnets* pg. 158.

Student Diary Assignment
- ☐ With the students, fill out the demonstration sheet found on SD pg. 119.

Nature Study: Seeds

This week, you will look at the different seeds in your neighborhood.

Preparation
- 📖 Read the pp. 458-459 (section on seed germination) in the *Handbook of Nature Study* to learn more about seeds.

Outdoor Time
- ☼ Go on a walk and collect the various seeds you find. Allow the students to make observations about the different types of seeds and their shapes and sizes. When you return home, plant some of your seeds in eggshell, as described in the *Handbook of Nature Study*. Afterward, have them make an entry into their nature journal.

Student Diary Assignment
- ☐ With the students, fill out the nature journal sheet found on SD pg. 121. The students can sketch what they have seen or you can write down their observations.

Read-Alouds

Optional Encyclopedia Pages
- 📖 *The Usborne Children's Encyclopedia* pp.94-95 How Plants Grow

Optional Library Books

- *The Magic School Bus Plants Seeds: A Book About How Living Things Grow* by Joanna Cole
- *Seeds* by Ken Robbins
- *A Fruit Is a Suitcase for Seeds* by Jean Richards and Anca Hariton
- *Curious George Plants a Seed* (Curious George Early Readers) by H. A. Rey

Coordinating Activities

These following activities will help you to reinforce the week's topic and main idea.

- **Art** – (Seed Prints) Have a plate with red paint on it for the students to use. Cut an apple in half horizontally instead of vertically so that the seed pods will create a star pattern. Have the students dip the apple half in the paint and use it to stamp a design on the paper.

    Student Diary Assignment
    - Have the students use SD pg. 120 to complete this activity.

    Lapbook Assignment
    - Have the students add the page they stamped to the "My Botany Projects" pocket in the lapbook.

- **Snack** – (Edible Seeds) Explain to the students that we can eat many different types of seeds and that we also eat fruits, which contain seeds. Have several types of fruit and seeds, such as cherry tomatoes, strawberries, blackberries, sunflower seeds, and pumpkin seeds. Enjoy trying the different fruits and seeds as you talk about how they look and taste different.

Notes

Possible Schedules for Week 3

Two Days a Week Schedule	
Day 1	Day 2
❑ Read the introduction with the students. Color the main idea page. ❑ Complete the Hands-on Project "Upside-down Plant" and fill out the demonstration sheet.	❑ Complete the Hands-on Project: Nature Study "Seeds" and fill out the nature journal sheet. ❑ Do the "Seed Prints" activity.
Supplies Needed for the Week ✓ Day 1: Lima bean seed (soaked overnight), Bean seeds, Ziploc baggy, Paper towel, Water ✓ Day 2: Collected seeds, Eggshell, Red paint, Apple, Plate, Paper	

Five Days a Week Schedule				
Day 1	Day 2	Day 3	Day 4	Day 5
❑ Read the introduction with the students. Color the main idea page. ❑ Eat "Edible Seeds" for snack.	❑ Complete the Hands-on Project "Upside-down Plant" and fill out the demonstration sheet. ❑ Read the selected pages in *The Usborne Children's Encyclopedia*.	❑ Complete the Seeds Mini-book. ❑ Choose one of the books from the read-aloud suggestions and read it to the students.	❑ Do the "Seed Prints" activity. ❑ Choose one of the books from the read-aloud suggestions and read it to the students.	❑ Complete the Hands-on Project: Nature Study "Seeds" and fill out the nature journal sheet.
Supplies Needed for the Week ✓ Day 1: Lima bean seed (soaked overnight), Several different fruits and seeds to eat ✓ Day 2: Bean seeds, Ziploc baggy, Paper towel, Water ✓ Day 4: Red paint, Apple, Plate, Paper ✓ Day 5: Collected seeds, Eggshell				

Leaves ~ Week 4

Weekly Topic

Main Idea
- Leaves help the plant to make food.

Introduction

Have a bean plant on the table in front of you. Say to the students:

We can see several parts of the bean plant here above the soil.

? *Can you name any of those parts?*

That's great, we can easily see the stem, flowers, and the leaves. Leaves are the part of the plant that are responsible for making the plants food.

Leaves have a special pigment in them called chlorophyll, which makes the leaves green. The pigment's job is to take in sunlight and convert it into energy that the plant can use to make food.

This week, we are going to take a closer look at leaves.

You may want to pull a leaf off of the plant and allow the students to observe it up close.

Student Diary Assignment
- Have the students color the coloring page found on SD pg. 122.

Lapbook Assignment
- Have the students cut out and color the Leaves Mini-book on LT pg. 50. You can have them cut out the main idea graphic included and glue it in the interior of the mini-book or you can write a sentence with what they have learned from the week for them on the inside of the mini-book. Once the students are done, have them glue the booklet into the mini-lapbook.

Hands-on Projects

Scientific Demonstration: Leaf Cover-up

In this demonstration, you will help the students to see how sunlight is an important part of photosynthesis.

Materials Needed
- ✓ Bean plant
- ✓ Paper
- ✓ Paper clip

Steps to Complete
1. Choose a leaf on your bean plant.
2. Cut out a 1-inch strip of paper long enough to fold over your leaf so that it covers both sides.
3. Use the paper clip to firmly attach the paper to your leaf so that it covers a portion of the leaf, but not all of it.
4. Let the plant sit in the sun for 3 to 4 days.
5. After several days take off the piece of paper. The section of the leaf that was covered should have turned yellow.

Explanation

This is because the chlorophyll in the leaf has moved out of that section to a place where it is able to continue to absorb sunlight and make energy for the plant.

Student Diary Assignment
- ☐ With the students, fill out the demonstration sheet found on SD pg. 123.

Nature Study: Leaves

This week, you will look at the different leaves in your neighborhood.

Preparation
- Read the pp. 626-627 (section on making leaf prints) in the *Handbook of Nature Study* to learn more about making leaf prints.

Outdoor Time
- Go on a walk and collect the various leaves you find. Allow the students to make observations about the different types of leaves, their shapes and sizes. When you return home make leaf prints, as described in the *Handbook of Nature Study*, into their nature journal.

Student Diary Assignment
- ☐ With the students, fill out the nature journal sheet found on SD pg. 125. The students can sketch what they have seen or you can write down their observations.

Read-Alouds

Optional Encyclopedia Pages
- *The Usborne Children's Encyclopedia* pg. 97 Leaves

Optional Library Books
- *Leaves* (Plant Parts series) (Pebble Plus: Plant Parts) by Vijaya Bodach,
- *I Am A Leaf* (Level 1 - Hello Reader) by Jean Marzollo and Judith Moffatt
- *Leaves* by David Ezra Stein

Coordinating Activities

These following activities will help you to reinforce the week's topic and main idea.

- **Art** – (Leaf Rubbings) Go outside and collect a few leaves. Once inside have the students lay out a leaf design under piece of paper. Then, have the students rub the side of a crayon over it to make a beautiful leaf rubbing design.

  Student Diary Assignment
  - Have the students use SD pg. 124 to complete this activity.

  Lapbook Assignment
  - Have the students add the page the colored to the "My Botany Projects" pocket in the lapbook.

- **Snack** – (Edible Leaves) Explain to the students that we can eat many different types of leaves. Have several types of leaves they can eat, such as lettuce, spinach, kale, or bok choy, along with some ranch dressing. Enjoy trying the leaves after dipping them in ranch dressing as you talk about their different looks and tastes.

- **More Fun** – (Where does the green go?) Do another activity from *More Mudpies to Magnets*, "100% Sun block: Where does the green go" on pg. 147, with the students. This demonstration will help the students to preserve a flower. You will need a sheet of cardboard for this activity.

Notes

Possible Schedules for Week 4

Two Days a Week Schedule	
Day 1	Day 2
❏ Read the introduction with the students. Color the main idea page. ❏ Complete the Hands-on Project "Leaf Cover-up" and fill out the demonstration sheet.	❏ Complete the Hands-on Project: Nature Study "Leaves" and fill out the nature journal sheet. ❏ Do the "Leaf Rubbings" activity.
Supplies Needed for the Week ✓ Day 1: Bean plant, Paper, Paper clip ✓ Day 2: Leaves, Paint, Crayons, Paper	

Five Days a Week Schedule				
Day 1	Day 2	Day 3	Day 4	Day 5
❏ Read the introduction with the students. Color the main idea page. ❏ Eat "Edible Leaves" for snack.	❏ Complete the Hands-on Project "Leaf Cover-up" and fill out the demonstration sheet. ❏ Read the selected pages in *The Usborne Children's Encyclopedia*.	❏ Have some more fun with the "Where does the green go" activity. ❏ Complete the Leaves Mini-book. ❏ Choose one of the books from the read-aloud suggestions and read it to the students.	❏ Do the "Leaf Rubbings" activity. ❏ Choose one of the books from the read-aloud suggestions and read it to the students.	❏ Complete the Hands-on Project: Nature Study "Leaves" and fill out the nature journal sheet.
Supplies Needed for the Week ✓ Day 1: Bean plant, Edible leaves (lettuce, spinach, kale or bok choy), Ranch dressing ✓ Day 2: Bean plant, Paper, Paper clip ✓ Day 3: Sheet of cardboard ✓ Day 4: Leaves, Crayons, Paper ✓ Day 5: Leaves, Paint, Paper				

Stems ~ Week 5

Weekly Topic

Main Idea
- The stem of a plant acts as its highway.

Introduction
Have a piece of celery and a magnifying glass out on the table in front of you. Say to the students:

This piece of celery is actually the stem of a plant. Let's take a closer look using this magnifying glass.

? Do you see the tubes running up the side of the piece of celery?

The job of these tubes is to carry water and nutrients up the plant and food down the plant. In other words, the stem acts as the highway of the plant, moving things around to where they need to be quickly.

This week, we are going to spend some more time looking at stems.

Allow the students to have some more time to look at the piece of celery with their magnifying glasses.

Student Diary Assignment
- Have the students color the coloring page found on SD pg. 126.

Lapbook Assignment
- Have the students cut out and color the Stem Mini-book on LT pg. 51. You can have them cut out the main idea graphic included and glue it in the interior of the mini-book or you can write a sentence with what they have learned from the week for them on the inside of the mini-book. Once the students are done, have them glue the booklet into the mini-lapbook.

Hands-on Projects

Scientific Demonstration: Thirsty Stems
In this demonstration, you will help the students to see how stems transport water in a plant.

Materials Needed
- ✓ Celery (with leaves)
- ✓ Food coloring
- ✓ Glass
- ✓ Water

Steps to Complete
1. Add several drops of food coloring to the water in a glass.
2. Place your piece of celery in the glass and set it aside for 3 days.
3. After several days, observe what has happened to your piece of celery. (*It should have turned the color of the water you put it in.*)

Explanation
The stem has transported the colored water throughout the plant.

Student Diary Assignment
- With the students, fill out the demonstration sheet found on SD pg. 127.

Nature Study: Oak Tree

This week, you are studying stems, which is a great time to look at trees since the trunk and branches of a tree are really giant stems. This week, your focus will be on oak trees.

Preparation
- Read the pp. 638-642 in the *Handbook of Nature Study* to learn more about oak trees.

Outdoor Time
- Go on a walk and look for oak trees. Allow the students to observe the tree and ask any questions they may have. You can use the information you have learned from reading the *Handbook of Nature Study* to answer their questions or to share information about what they are observing.

Student Diary Assignment
- With the students, fill out the nature journal sheet found on SD pg. 129. The students can sketch what they have seen or you can write down their observations.

Read-Alouds

Optional Encyclopedia Pages
- *The Usborne Children's Encyclopedia* - There are no new pages scheduled.

Optional Library Books
- *Stems* (Plant Parts) by Vijaya Bodach
- *Plant Stems & Roots* (Look Once, Look Again Science Series) by David M. Schwartz
- *Stems* (First Step Nonfiction) by Melanie Mitchell

Coordinating Activities

These following activities will help you to reinforce the week's topic and main idea.

- **Art** – (Blowing Stems) Mix a little brown or green paint with some water to dilute the paint a bit. Place a large drop of the watered-down paint at the bottom of a sheet of paper. Then, have the students use a straw to blow the drop of paint into stems. Allow it to dry before adding leaves and flowers to the plants.

   Student Diary Assignment
   - Have the students use SD pg. 128 to complete this activity.

   Lapbook Assignment
   - Have the students add the page they painted to the "My Botany Projects" pocket in the lapbook.

- **Snack** – (Edible Stems) Explain that celery is a stem we can eat! Serve celery sticks filled with cream cheese for snack.

Notes

Possible Schedules for Week 5

Two Days a Week Schedule

Day 1	Day 2
❑ Read the introduction with the students. Color the main idea page. ❑ Complete the Hands-on Project "Thirsty Stems" and fill out the demonstration sheet.	❑ Complete the Hands-on Project: Nature Study "Oak Tree" and fill out the nature journal sheet. ❑ Do the "Blowing Stems" activity.

Supplies Needed for the Week
- ✓ Day 1: Celery (with leaves), Magnifying glass, Food coloring, Glass, Water
- ✓ Day 2: Brown and green paint, Straw, Water, Paper

Five Days a Week Schedule

Day 1	Day 2	Day 3	Day 4	Day 5
❑ Read the introduction with the students. Color the main idea page. ❑ Eat "Edible Stems" for snack.	❑ Complete the Hands-on Project "Thirsty Stems" and fill out the demonstration sheet. ❑ Choose one of the books from the read-aloud suggestions and read it to the students.	❑ Complete the Stems Mini-book. ❑ Choose one of the books from the read-aloud suggestions and read it to the students.	❑ Do the "Blowing Stems" activity. ❑ Choose one of the books from the read-aloud suggestions and read it to the students.	❑ Complete the Hands-on Project: Nature Study "Oak Tree" and fill out the nature journal sheet.

Supplies Needed for the Week
- ✓ Day 1: Celery, Magnifying glass, Celery Sticks, Cream Cheese
- ✓ Day 2: Celery (with leaves), Food coloring, Glass, Water
- ✓ Day 4: Brown and green paint, Straw, Water, Paper

Roots ~ Week 6

Weekly Topic

Main Idea
- Roots take in water and nutrients from the soil.

Introduction

Have a green onion, complete with roots, out on the table in front of you. Say to the students:

This green onion still has its roots on it.

Point out the roots to the students and allow them to observe the roots for a moment before continuing.

Normally, the roots of a plant are underground. This is because their job is to absorb water and nutrients from the soil. The plant then transports these ingredients through the stems and into the leaves to make food for the plant.

This week, we are going to take a closer look at roots.

You may also want to dig up the bean plant you planted earlier in this unit to examine its roots.

Student Diary Assignment
- Have the students color the coloring page found on SD pg. 130.

Lapbook Assignment
- Have the students cut out and color the Roots Mini-book on LT pg. 52. You can have them cut out the main idea graphic included and glue it in the interior of the mini-book or you can write a sentence with what they have learned from the week for them on the inside of the mini-book. Once the students are done, have them glue the booklet into the mini-lapbook.

Hands-on Projects

Scientific Demonstration: Hydroponics

In this demonstration, you will help the students to see up close how the roots of a plant grow.

Materials Needed
- ✓ Clear plastic cups
- ✓ Cardboard
- ✓ Sprouted plant (basil or lettuce plants work well for hydroponics)
- ✓ Cotton
- ✓ Liquid plant food
- ✓ Water

Steps to Complete
1. Follow the directions found on *More Mudpies to Magnets* pg. 151.

Student Diary Assignment
- ☐ With the students, fill out the demonstration sheet found on SD pg. 131.

Nature Study: Maple Tree

This week, you are studying roots. Since roots are hard to study without digging up lots of plants, you will study another type of tree this week.

Preparation
- Read the pp. 628-633 in the *Handbook of Nature Study* to learn more about maple trees.

Outdoor Time
- Go on a walk and look for maple trees. Allow the students to observe the tree and ask any questions they may have. You can use the information you have learned from reading the *Handbook of Nature Study* to answer their questions or to share information about what they are observing.

Student Diary Assignment
- ☐ With the students, fill out the nature journal sheet found on SD pg. 133. The students can sketch what they have seen or you can write down their observations.

Read-Alouds

Optional Encyclopedia Pages
- *The Usborne Children's Encyclopedia* - There are no new pages scheduled.

Optional Library Books
- *Roots* (First Step Nonfiction) by Melanie Mitchell
- *Roots* (Plant Parts series) (Pebble Plus: Plant Parts) by Vijaya Bodach

📖 *Plant Plumbing: A Book About Roots and Stems* by Susan Blackaby

Coordinating Activities

These following activities will help you to reinforce the week's topic and main idea.

✂ Art – (Painting with Roots) Use the green onion you examined in the introduction as a paintbrush. Allow the students to create their own masterpiece using their root-brush!

Student Diary Assignment
▫ Have the students use SD pg. 132 to complete this activity.

Lapbook Assignment
📁 Have the students add the page they painted to the "My Botany Projects" pocket in the lapbook.

✂ Snack – (Edible Roots) Explain that we eat several different types of roots. These include potatoes, carrots, radishes, and other root vegetables. Serve carrot sticks or shoestring potato sticks for snack that day.

✂ Field Trip – (Greenhouse) Wrap up your plant studies by taking a field trip to a greenhouse. While you are there look for the different parts of the plant that you have learned about during this botany unit.

Notes

Possible Schedules for Week 6

Two Days a Week Schedule

Day 1	Day 2
❑ Read the introduction with the students. Color the main idea page. ❑ Complete the Hands-on Project "Hydroponics" and fill out the demonstration sheet.	❑ Complete the Hands-on Project: Nature Study "Tree Roots" and fill out the nature journal sheet. ❑ Do the "Painting with Roots" activity.

Supplies Needed for the Week
- ✓ Day 1: Green onion with roots, Clear plastic cups, Cardboard, Sprouted plant (basil or lettuce plants work well for hydroponics), Cotton, Liquid plant food, Water
- ✓ Day 2: Green onion with roots, Paint, Paper

Five Days a Week Schedule

Day 1	Day 2	Day 3	Day 4	Day 5
❑ Read the introduction with the students. Color the main idea page. ❑ Eat "Edible Roots" for snack.	❑ Complete the Hands-on Project "Hydroponics" and fill out the demonstration sheet. ❑ Choose one of the books from the read-aloud suggestions and read it to the students.	❑ Take a field trip to a greenhouse. ❑ Complete the Roots Mini-book.	❑ Do the "Painting with Roots" activity. ❑ Choose one of the books from the read-aloud suggestions and read it to the students.	❑ Complete the Hands-on Project: Nature Study "Tree Roots" and fill out the nature journal sheet.

Supplies Needed for the Week
- ✓ Day 1: Green onion with roots, Carrot sticks or shoestring potato sticks
- ✓ Day 2: Clear plastic cups, Cardboard, Sprouted plant (basil or lettuce plants work well for hydroponics), Cotton, Liquid plant food, Water
- ✓ Day 4: Green onion with roots, Paint, Paper

Intro to Science
Unit 6: Intro to Zoology

Intro to Zoology Unit Overview

Sequence for Study
- Week 1: Fish
- Week 2: Insects
- Week 3: Invertebrates
- Week 4: Mammals
- Week 5: Reptiles
- Week 6: Birds

Supplies Needed for the Unit

Week	Introduction Props	Hands-on Project Materials	Coordinating Activities Supplies
1	Pictures of Fish	Small fish bowl, Water filter, Aquarium rocks, Goldfish	Goldfish crackers, Fish outline on paper, Watercolor paints, Glitter
2	Butterfly Life Cycle Cards from Appendix	Fly (or butterfly), Glass jar with lid, Ice, Cake pan	Lettuce, Eyedropper, Paint, Paper, Glitter, Sequins, Glue, Butterfly outline on paper
3	Pictures of invertebrates	Earthworms, Shady outdoor area	Gummy worms, Collection jar or bag, Film canisters, Magnifying glass, Paint, Thick string, Paper
4	Pictures of Animals	Animal pictures or models	Animal crackers, Mammal pictures from old magazines or animal stickers
5	Pictures of reptiles	Thermometer	Peanut butter, Powdered milk, Honey, Cocoa, Vanilla, Chopped Nuts, Raisins, Mini M&M's, Pictures of reptiles, 2 Colors of paint, Paper, Black Marker
6	Pictures of birds	Clean, cooked chicken bones, Chicken skeleton sketch (in the Appendix)	Mangoes, blueberries, or strawberries, Sunflower seeds, Bird feeder, Feathers, Paint, Paper

Books Scheduled

Hands-on Projects (Required Books)
- *More Mudpies to Magnets (If you are using the scientific demonstration option.)*
- *Handbook of Nature Study (If you are using the nature study option.)*

Read-Aloud Suggestions

Optional Encyclopedia
- *The Usborne Children's Encyclopedia*

Week 1
- *What's It Like to Be a Fish?* (Let's-Read-and-Find... Science 1) by Wendy Pfeffer
- *Rainbow Fish Big Book* by Marcus Pfister Herbert and J. Alison James
- *Fish Eyes: A Book You Can Count On* by Lois Ehlert

Week 2
- *Butterfly House* by Eve Bunting and Greg Shed
- *A Butterfly Grows* (Green Light Readers Level 2) by Stephen R. Swinburne
- *From Caterpillar to Butterfly: Following the Life Cycle* by Suzanne Slade
- *The Life of a Butterfly* by Clare Hibbert

Week 3
- *No Backbone! the World of Invertebrates* by Natalie Lunis
- *I Wonder What It's Like to Be an Earthworm* (Hovanec, Erin M. Life Science Wonder Series.) by Erin M. Hovanec
- *Are You a Snail?* (Backyard Books) by Judy Allen

Week 4
- *About Mammals: A Guide For Children* by Cathryn Sill and John Sill
- *Eye Wonder: Mammals* (Eye Wonder) by Sarah Walker
- *Is a Camel a Mammal?* by Tish Rabe and Jim Durk
- *Animals Called Mammals* (What Kind of Animal Is It?) by Bobbie Kalman

Week 5
- *Miles and Miles of Reptiles: All About Reptiles* by Tish Rabe and Aristides Ruiz
- *Eye Wonder: Reptiles* (Eye Wonder) by Simon Holland
- *Reptiles* (True Books : Animals) by Melissa Stewart
- *Fun Facts About Snakes!* (I Like Reptiles and Amphibians!) by Carmen Bredeson

Week 6
- *About Birds: A Guide for Children* by Cathryn Sill and John Sill
- *Fine Feathered Friends: All About Birds* by Tish Rabe
- *How Do Birds Find Their Way?* (Let's-Read-and-Find... Science 2) by Roma Gans
- *The Magic School Bus Flies from the Nest* by Joanna Cole and Carolyn Bracken

Fish ~ Week 1

Weekly Topic

Main Idea
- Fish have gills so they can breathe underwater.

Introduction
Have pictures of fish out on the table in front of you. Say to the students:

During this unit, we are going to look at several different types of animals. This week, we are going to look at fish.

? *What do you know about fish?*

Let the students answer, correcting any false information and agreeing with correct facts. Then say to the students:

That's great!

All fish have gills so that they can breathe underwater. Fish also have scales all over their body and they have fins instead of legs and arms to help them move through the water.

Fish are cold-blooded, which means that they don't produce their own heat like we mammals do. This week, we are going to learn more about fish!

Student Diary Assignment
- Have the students color the coloring page found on SD pg. 136.

Lapbook Assignment
- Have the students cut out and color the Fish Mini-book on LT pg. 57. You can have them cut out the main idea graphic included and glue it in the interior of the mini-book or you can write a sentence with what they have learned from the week for them on the inside of the mini-book. Once the students are done, have them glue the booklet into the mini-lapbook.

Hands-on Projects

Scientific Demonstration: Goldfish Tank

In this demonstration, you will help the students to see what fish do.

Materials Needed
- ✓ Small fish bowl
- ✓ Water filter
- ✓ Aquarium rocks
- ✓ Goldfish

Steps to Complete
1. For this week's demonstration, you will set up a goldfish tank if you do not already have one to observe. View this website for more detailed instructions on how to set up a goldfish tank:
   - https://www.cuteness.com/article/set-up-goldfish-bowl
2. Once the tank is set up, have the students observe the goldfish's behavior.

Student Diary Assignment
- With the students, fill out the demonstration sheet found on SD pg. 137.

Nature Study: Fish

This week, you will look at fish found in your area.

Preparation
- Read the pp. 144-169 in the *Handbook of Nature Study* to learn more about fish. If you're lucky enough to live near a brook or stream, you can read about all the fish found in your area from the section. If not, just concentrate on the goldfish section found on pp. 144-147.

Outdoor Time
- Go on a walk and look for a brook, stream or pond with fish in it to observe. Allow the students to observe the fish and ask any questions they may have. You can use the information you have learned from reading the *Handbook of Nature Study* to answer their questions or to share information about what they are observing. If you cannot find fish to observe use a goldfish for your nature study time.

Student Diary Assignment
- With the students, fill out the nature journal sheet found on SD pg. 139. The students can sketch what they have seen or you can write down their observations.

Read-Alouds

Optional Encyclopedia Pages
- *The Usborne Children's Encyclopedia* pp. 80-81 (Underwater Life)

Optional Library Books

- *What's It Like to Be a Fish?* (Let's-Read-and-Find... Science 1) by Wendy Pfeffer and Holly Keller
- *Rainbow Fish Big Book* by Marcus Pfister Herbert and J. Alison James
- *Fish Eyes: A Book You Can Count On* by Lois Ehlert

Coordinating Activities

These following activities will help you to reinforce the week's topic and main idea.

- **Art** – (Sparkle Fish) Give the students a black-line image or hand-drawn outline of a fish. Have them use watercolor paints to paint their own rainbow fish. Then, you can have them decorate it with glitter and other sparkly things.

Student Diary Assignment
- Have the students use SD pg. 138 to complete this activity.

Lapbook Assignment
- Have the students cut out the "My Zoology Projects" pocket on LT pg. 63. Have them glue the pocket into the lapbook and add the fish project they just did to the pocket.

- **Snack** – (Goldfish crackers) Have some goldfish crackers for snack time this week.
- **Field Trip** – (Aquarium) Go on a field trip to an aquarium to observe fish.

Notes

Possible Schedules for Week 1

Two Days a Week Schedule	
Day 1	Day 2
❏ Read the introduction with the students. Color the main idea page. ❏ Complete the Hands-on Project "Goldfish Tank" and fill out the demonstration sheet.	❏ Complete the Hands-on Project: Nature Study "Fish" and fill out the nature journal sheet. ❏ Do the "Sparkle Fish" activity.
Supplies Needed for the Week ✓ Day 1: Pictures of Fish, Small fish bowl, Water filter, Aquarium rocks, Goldfish ✓ Day 2: Fish outline on paper, Watercolor paints, Glitter	

Five Days a Week Schedule				
Day 1	Day 2	Day 3	Day 4	Day 5
❏ Read the introduction with the students. Color the main idea page. ❏ Eat "Goldfish" for snack.	❏ Complete the Hands-on Project "Goldfish Tank" and fill out the demonstration sheet. ❏ Read the selected pages in *The Usborne Children's Encyclopedia*.	❏ Go on a field trip to an aquarium. ❏ Complete the Fish Mini-book. ❏ Choose one of the books from the read-aloud suggestions and read it to the students.	❏ Do the "Sparkle Fish" activity. ❏ Choose one of the books from the read-aloud suggestions and read it to the students.	❏ Complete the Hands-on Project: Nature Study "Fish" and fill out the nature journal sheet.
Supplies Needed for the Week ✓ Day 1: Pictures of Fish, Goldfish crackers ✓ Day 2: Small fish bowl, Water filter, Aquarium rocks, Goldfish ✓ Day 4: Fish outline on paper, Watercolor paints, Glitter				

Butterflies ~ Week 2

Weekly Topic

Main Idea
- Caterpillars make a chrysalis and then come out as a butterfly.

Introduction
Have the life cycle of a butterfly project pictures out on the table in front of you. (*You can find these pictures on pg. 191 of the Appendix.*) Say to the students:

We are going to look at the life cycle of a butterfly this week. These cards show the cycle in four steps.

Read each of the cards to your students, pointing to each one as you go through them. Then, say to the students:

After the cycle is the complete the mature butterflies go and lay more eggs to begin the cycle again.

This week, we are going to look at butterflies.

You can have the students color the life cycle cards and glue them onto a sheet of construction paper to make a poster for their room.

Student Diary Assignment
- Have the students color the coloring page found on SD pg. 140.

Lapbook Assignment
- Have the students cut out and color the Butterfly Mini-book on LT pg. 58. You can have them cut out the main idea graphic included and glue it in the interior of the mini-book or you can write a sentence with what they have learned from the week for them on the inside of the mini-book. Once the students are done, have them glue the booklet into the mini-lapbook.

Hands-on Projects

Scientific Demonstration: Cool off a fly

In this demonstration, you will help the students to see how temperature changes affect insects.

Materials Needed
- ✓ Fly (or butterfly)
- ✓ Glass jar with lid
- ✓ Ice
- ✓ Cake pan

Steps to Complete
1. Follow the directions found on *More Mudpies to Magnets* pg. 167.

Student Diary Assignment
- ☐ With the students, fill out the demonstration sheet found on SD pg. 141.

Nature Study: Butterflies

This week, you will look at the butterflies found in your area.

Preparation
- Read the pp. 301-309 in the *Handbook of Nature Study* to learn more about the Black Swallowtail and Monarch butterflies. If these butterflies don't visit your area, choose one of the other butterflies.

Outdoor Time
- Go on a walk and look for butterflies to observe. Allow the students to observe the butterflies and ask any questions they may have. You can use the information you have learned from reading the *Handbook of Nature Study* to answer their questions or to share information about what they are observing.

Student Diary Assignment
- ☐ With the students, fill out the nature journal sheet found on SD pg. 143. The students can sketch what they have seen or you can write down their observations.

Read-Alouds

Optional Encyclopedia Pages
- *The Usborne Children's Encyclopedia* pp. 76-77 (Butterflies)

Optional Library Books
- *Butterfly House* by Eve Bunting and Greg Shed
- *A Butterfly Grows* (Green Light Readers Level 2) by Stephen R. Swinburne
- *From Caterpillar to Butterfly: Following the Life Cycle* by Suzanne Slade
- *The Life of a Butterfly* by Clare Hibbert

Coordinating Activities

These following activities will help you to reinforce the week's topic and main idea.

- **Art** – (Butterfly Beauty) Have the students color and decorate with glitter and sequins a black-line or hand-drawn outline of a butterfly.

  Student Diary Assignment
  - Have the students use SD pg. __ to complete this activity.

  Lapbook Assignment
  - Have the students add the butterfly they decorated to the "My Zoology Projects" pocket in the lapbook.

- **Snack** – (Eat like a Caterpillar) Let the students pretend to be caterpillars eating leaves. Use lettuce for the leaves.

- **More Fun** – (Butterfly Symmetry) Using an eye dropper, have the students drop blobs of paint on one half of a piece of paper. Before the paint dries, have the students fold the paper in half and press so that the paint spreads out evenly on both sides. Then, cut out a half butterfly shape from the paper, using the middle fold line as the middle of your butterfly. Open it up and let it dry. Talk about how a butterfly has symmetry (i.e., the design of its wings are the same on both sides) just like the butterfly you just made.

Notes

Possible Schedules for Week 2

Two Days a Week Schedule

Day 1	Day 2
❑ Read the introduction with the students. Color the main idea page. ❑ Complete the Hands-on Project "Cool Off a Fly" and fill out the demonstration sheet.	❑ Complete the Hands-on Project: Nature Study "Butterflies" and fill out the nature journal sheet. ❑ Do the "Butterfly Beauty" activity.

Supplies Needed for the Week
- ✓ Day 1: Butterfly Life Cycle Cards from Appendix, Fly (or butterfly), Glass jar with lid, Ice, Cake pan
- ✓ Day 2: Glitter, Sequins, Glue, Butterfly outline on paper

Five Days a Week Schedule

Day 1	Day 2	Day 3	Day 4	Day 5
❑ Read the introduction with the students. Color the main idea page. ❑ Eat like a caterpillar for snack.	❑ Complete the Hands-on Project "Cool Off a Fly" and fill out the demonstration sheet. ❑ Read the selected pages in *The Usborne Children's Encyclopedia*.	❑ Have some more fun with the "Butterfly Symmetry" activity. ❑ Complete the Butterfly Mini-book. ❑ Choose one of the books from the read-aloud suggestions and read it to the students.	❑ Do the "Butterfly Beauty" activity. ❑ Choose one of the books from the read-aloud suggestions and read it to the students.	❑ Complete the Hands-on Project: Nature Study "Butterflies" and fill out the nature journal sheet.

Supplies Needed for the Week
- ✓ Day 1: Butterfly Life Cycle Cards from Appendix, Lettuce
- ✓ Day 2: Fly (or butterfly), Glass jar with lid, Ice, Cake pan
- ✓ Day 3: Eyedropper, Paint, Paper
- ✓ Day 4: Glitter, Sequins, Glue, Butterfly outline on paper

Invertebrates ~ Week 3

Weekly Topic

Main Idea

- Invertebrates, like snails and worms, have no backbones.

Introduction

Have pictures of invertebrates out on the table in front of you. Say to the students:

Humans are vertebrates because we have backbones. The human backbone is called the spine.

? *Can you find your spine?*

Have the students feel the backs of their necks to find their spines. Then say:

Good job! There are many animals that do have backbones like us, but there are also animals that do not have backbones. They are called invertebrates.

Pause to point out the pictures you have of invertebrates and name the animals before continuing:

This week, we are going to look closer at snails and worms, which are animals that have no backbones. Snails and worms are both invertebrates.

Student Diary Assignment

☐ Have the students color the coloring page found on SD pg. 144.

Lapbook Assignment

📁 Have the students cut out and color the Invertebrates Mini-book on LT pg. 59. You can have them cut out the main idea graphic included and glue it in the interior of the mini-book or you can write a sentence with what they have learned from the week for them on the inside of the mini-book. Once the students are done, have them glue the booklet into the mini-lapbook.

Hands-on Projects

Scientific Demonstration: Earthworm Grand Prix

In this demonstration, you will help the students to see how invertebrates move.

Materials Needed
- ✓ Earthworms
- ✓ Shady outdoor area

Steps to Complete
1. Follow the directions found on *More Mudpies to Magnets* pg. 171.

Student Diary Assignment
- ☐ With the students, fill out the demonstration sheet found on SD pg. 145.

Nature Study: Garden Snails

This week, you will look for garden snails in your backyard. Be sure to also point out any other invertebrates you run across, such as worms and insects.

Preparation
- Read the pp. 416-418 in the *Handbook of Nature Study* to learn more about invertebrates and the garden snail.

Outdoor Time
- Go on a walk and look for snails and other invertebrates to observe. Allow the students to observe them and ask any questions they may have. You can use the information you have learned from reading the *Handbook of Nature Study* to answer their questions or to share information about what they are observing.

Student Diary Assignment
- ☐ With the students, fill out the nature journal sheet found on SD pg. 147. The students can sketch what they have seen or you can write down their observations.

Read-Alouds

Optional Encyclopedia Pages
- *The Usborne Children's Encyclopedia* pp. 74-75 (Creepy Crawlies)

Optional Library Books
- *No Backbone! the World of Invertebrates* by Natalie Lunis
- *I Wonder What It's Like to Be an Earthworm* (Hovanec, Erin M. Life Science Wonder Series.) by Erin M. Hovanec
- *Are You a Snail?* (Backyard Books) by Judy Allen

Coordinating Activities

These following activities will help you to reinforce the week's topic and main idea.

✂ **Art** – (Worm Trails) Have the students drag a piece of thick string through paint. Then have them move the piece of string across a sheet of paper like a worm.

Student Diary Assignment
- Have the students use SD pg. 146 to complete this activity.

Lapbook Assignment
- Have the students add the page they painted to the "My Zoology Projects" pocket in the lapbook.

✂ **Snack** – (Edible Invertebrates) Serve the students escargot (snails). Just kidding! Tell the students that in other countries they do eat invertebrates, such as snails and crickets, but today we are going to eat worms. Then, serve them gummy worms!

✂ **More Fun** – (Invertebrate Safari) Do another activity from *More Mudpies to Magnets*, "Invertebrate Safari" on pg. 170, with the students. This demonstration will help the students to learn more about the different types of invertebrates. You will need a collection jar or bag, film canisters, and a magnifying glass for this activity.

Notes

Possible Schedules for Week 3

Two Days a Week Schedule	
Day 1	Day 2
❑ Read the introduction with the students. Color the main idea page. ❑ Complete the Hands-on Project "Earthworm Grand Prix" and fill out the demonstration sheet.	❑ Complete the Hands-on Project: Nature Study "Garden Snail" and fill out the nature journal sheet. ❑ Do the "Worm Trails" activity.
Supplies Needed for the Week ✓ Day 1: Pictures of invertebrates, Earthworms, Shady outdoor area ✓ Day 2: Paint, Thick string, Paper	

Five Days a Week Schedule				
Day 1	Day 2	Day 3	Day 4	Day 5
❑ Read the introduction with the students. Color the main idea page. ❑ Eat "Edible Invertebrates" for snack.	❑ Complete the Hands-on Project "Earthworm Grand Prix" and fill out the demonstration sheet. ❑ Read the selected pages in *The Usborne Children's Encyclopedia*.	❑ Have some more fun with the "Invertebrate Safari" activity. ❑ Complete the Invertebrates Mini-book. ❑ Choose one of the books from the read-aloud suggestions and read it to the students.	❑ Do the "Worm Trails" activity. ❑ Choose one of the books from the read-aloud suggestions and read it to the students.	❑ Complete the Hands-on Project: Nature Study "Garden Snail" and fill out the nature journal sheet.
Supplies Needed for the Week ✓ Day 1: Pictures of invertebrates, Gummy worms ✓ Day 2: Earthworms, Shady outdoor area ✓ Day 3: Collection jar or bag, Film canisters, Magnifying glass ✓ Day 4: Paint, Thick string, Paper				

Mammals ~ Week 4

Weekly Topic

Main Idea
- Mammals, like rabbits, have fur or hair.

Introduction
Have pictures of mammals out on the table in front of you. Say to the students:

Mammals are animals that have fur or hair. These animals also feed their young with milk. Did you know that we are mammals?

? *Can you think of some other mammals?*

Let the students share their ideas. *(If the students are unsure, have them look at the pictures you have of mammals and name those.)* Then say:

Those are great ideas! Rabbits are also mammals. They have fur and they feed their babies milk. They are also warm-blooded, which means that they can make their own heat to keep their bodies warm.

This week, we are going to look at different types of mammals and learn more about how they compare to us.

Student Diary Assignment
- Have the students color the coloring page found on SD pg. 148.

Lapbook Assignment
- Have the students cut out and color the Mammals Mini-book on LT pg. 60. You can have them cut out the main idea graphic included and glue it in the interior of the mini-book or you can write a sentence with what they have learned from the week for them on the inside of the mini-book. Once the students are done, have them glue the booklet into the mini-lapbook.

Hands-on Projects

Scientific Demonstration: Compare Me to Them

In this demonstration, you will help the students to see how different mammals compare to human beings.

Materials Needed
- ✓ Animal pictures or models

Steps to Complete
1. Follow the directions found on *More Mudpies to Magnets* pg. 172-173.

Student Diary Assignment
- ☐ With the students, fill out the demonstration sheet found on SD pg. 149.

Nature Study: Rabbits

This week, you will look for rabbits in your backyard. Be sure to also point out any other mammals you run across, such as squirrels, dogs, and cats.

Preparation
- 📖 Read the pp. 214-218 in the *Handbook of Nature Study* to learn more about mammals and rabbits.

Outdoor Time
- ☼ Go on a walk and look for rabbits or other mammals to observe. Allow the students to observe them and ask any questions they may have. You can use the information you have learned from reading the *Handbook of Nature Study* to answer their questions or to share information about what they are observing.

Student Diary Assignment
- ☐ With the students, fill out the nature journal sheet found on SD pg. 151. The students can sketch what they have seen or you can write down their observations.

Read-Alouds

Optional Encyclopedia Pages
- 📖 *The Usborne Children's Encyclopedia* pp. 60-61 (Mammals)

Optional Library Books
- 📖 *About Mammals: A Guide For Children* by Cathryn Sill and John Sill
- 📖 *Eye Wonder: Mammals* (Eye Wonder) by Sarah Walker
- 📖 *Is a Camel a Mammal?* by Tish Rabe and Jim Durk
- 📖 *Animals Called Mammals* (What Kind of Animal Is It?) by Bobbie Kalman and Kristina Lundblad

Coordinating Activities

These following activities will help you to reinforce the week's topic and main idea.

✂ **Art** – (Mammal Collage) Have the students cut out pictures of mammals from old magazines or use animal stickers that you have purchased. Have them make a collage of mammals on a sheet of paper.

Student Diary Assignment
- Have the students use SD pg. 150 to complete this activity.

Lapbook Assignment
- Have the students add the collage to the "My Zoology Projects" pocket in the lapbook.

✂ **Snack** – (Animal Crackers) Have animal crackers for snack one day. Talk about the different kinds of animals you find, what kind of hair, teeth, hands, and noses they have. Also discuss what they eat. (*Note – You could also introduce the concept of herbivores, which eat plants, omnivores, which eat both plants and meat, and carnivores, which eat meat.*)

✂ **Game** – (Mammal Classification) Collect pictures of various types of mammals. Have the students separate them into categories that they choose. Some possibilities are to sort by color, by teeth, by where they live, or by what they eat.

Notes

Possible Schedules for Week 4

Two Days a Week Schedule	
Day 1	Day 2
❑ Read the introduction with the students. Color the main idea page. ❑ Complete the Hands-on Project "Compare Me to Them" and fill out the demonstration sheet.	❑ Complete the Hands-on Project: Nature Study "Rabbits" and fill out the nature journal sheet. ❑ Do the "Mammal Collage" activity.
Supplies Needed for the Week ✓ Day 1: Animal pictures or models ✓ Day 2: Mammal pictures from old magazines or animal stickers	

Five Days a Week Schedule				
Day 1	Day 2	Day 3	Day 4	Day 5
❑ Read the introduction with the students. Color the main idea page. ❑ Eat "Animal Crackers" for snack.	❑ Complete the Hands-on Project "Compare Me to Them" and fill out the demonstration sheet. ❑ Read the selected pages in *The Usborne Children's Encyclopedia*.	❑ Play a game of "Mammal Classification." ❑ Complete the Mammals Mini-book. ❑ Choose one of the books from the read-aloud suggestions and read it to the students.	❑ Do the "Mammal Collage" activity. ❑ Choose one of the books from the read-aloud suggestions and read it to the students.	❑ Complete the Hands-on Project: Nature Study "Rabbits" and fill out the nature journal sheet.
Supplies Needed for the Week ✓ Day 1: Pictures of Animals, Animal crackers ✓ Day 2: Animal pictures or models ✓ Day 3: Pictures of Animals ✓ Day 4: Mammal pictures from old magazines or animal stickers				

Reptiles ~ Week 5

Weekly Topic

Main Idea

- Reptiles, like snakes, are cold-blooded.

Introduction

Have pictures of reptiles out on the table in front of you. Say to the students:

Reptiles, like snakes, are cold-blooded animals, just like fish.

? *Do you remember what it means to be cold-blooded?*

That's right! Cold-blooded animals take on the temperature of their surroundings because they don't make their own heat. This means that they are hot when their surroundings are hot and cold when their surroundings are cold. All reptiles, including snakes, are cold-blooded.

This week, we are going to look at reptiles.

Have the students color the page found in the student workbook on pg. 109.

Student Diary Assignment

- Have the students color the coloring page found on SD pg. 152.

Lapbook Assignment

- Have the students cut out and color the Reptiles Mini-book on LT pg. 61. You can have them cut out the main idea graphic included and glue it in the interior of the mini-book or you can write a sentence with what they have learned from the week for them on the inside of the mini-book. Once the students are done, have them glue the booklet into the mini-lapbook.

Hands-on Projects

Scientific Demonstration: Cold-Blooded

In this demonstration, you will help the students to see how temperature affects reptiles.

Materials Needed
- ✓ Thermometer

Steps to Complete
1. Place the thermometer in the sun. Read the thermometer after 2 minutes. (*The temperature should have increased rapidly.*)
2. Then, place the thermometer in the shade. Read the thermometer after 2 minutes. (*The temperature should have dropped significantly.*)

Explanation
Explain to the students that the thermometer is like a cold-blooded animal. Their temperature changes very quickly depending on whether they are in the sun or in the shade. So, if a snake wants to warm up, he sits out in the sun. If he wants to cool off, he curls up in the shade.

Student Diary Assignment
- With the students, fill out the demonstration sheet found on SD pg. 153.

Nature Study: Reptiles

This week, you will look for reptiles, such as lizards, in your backyard. (If you do find snakes, do not handle them!)

Preparation
- Read the pp. 193-194 in the *Handbook of Nature Study* to learn more about reptiles. You may want to skim the remaining sections to learn more about specific reptiles in your area.

Outdoor Time
- Go on a walk and look for reptiles (such as lizards) to observe. Allow the students to observe them and ask any questions they may have. You can use the information you have learned from reading the *Handbook of Nature Study* to answer their questions or to share information about what they are observing.

Student Diary Assignment
- With the students, fill out the nature journal sheet found on SD pg. 155. The students can sketch what they have seen or you can write down their observations.

Read-Alouds

Optional Encyclopedia Pages
- *The Usborne Children's Encyclopedia* pp. 70-71 (Reptile Life)

Optional Library Books

- *Miles and Miles of Reptiles: All About Reptiles* by Tish Rabe and Aristides Ruiz
- *Eye Wonder: Reptiles* (Eye Wonder) by Simon Holland
- *Reptiles* (True Books : Animals) by Melissa Stewart
- *Fun Facts About Snakes!* (I Like Reptiles and Amphibians!) by Carmen Bredeson

Coordinating Activities

These following activities will help you to reinforce the week's topic and main idea.

Art – (Fingerprint Snake) See this website for directions:
http://www.dltk-kids.com/crafts/miscellaneous/fingerprint_snake.htm

Student Diary Assignment
- Have the students use SD pg. 154 to complete this activity.

Lapbook Assignment
- Have the students add their fingerprint snakes to the "My Zoology Projects" pocket in the lapbook.

Snack – (Chocolate Snakes) You will need ½ cup peanut butter, ½ cup powdered milk, ½ cup honey, 1 tbsp cocoa, ½ tsp vanilla, ½ cup chopped nuts, ½ cup raisins, and mini M&M's. (**Note** – *If you students are allergic to peanuts, substitute another nut butter.*) Combine the peanut butter and the powdered milk until blended. Stir in honey, cocoa, vanilla, nuts, and raisins - in that order. Roll your mixture into small snake shapes and add 2 mini M&M's for eyes using peanut butter to attach the candies. Place the snakes on wax paper on a cookie sheet and chill in the refrigerator until very firm.

Game – (Reptile Classification) Collect pictures of various types of reptiles. Have the students separate them into categories that they choose. Some possibilities are to sort by color, by where they live, or by what they eat.

Notes

Possible Schedules for Week 5

Two Days a Week Schedule	
Day 1	Day 2
❑ Read the introduction with the students. Color the main idea page. ❑ Complete the Hands-on Project "Cold-blooded" and fill out the demonstration sheet.	❑ Complete the Hands-on Project: Nature Study "Reptiles" and fill out the nature journal sheet. ❑ Do the "Fingerprint Snakes" activity.
Supplies Needed for the Week ✓ Day 1: Pictures of reptiles, Thermometer ✓ Day 2: 2 Colors of paint, Paper, Black Marker	

Five Days a Week Schedule				
Day 1	Day 2	Day 3	Day 4	Day 5
❑ Read the introduction with the students. Color the main idea page. ❑ Eat "Chocolate Snakes" for snack.	❑ Complete the Hands-on Project "Cold-blooded" and fill out the demonstration sheet. ❑ Read the selected pages in *The Usborne Children's Encyclopedia*.	❑ Play a game of "Reptile Classification." ❑ Complete the Reptiles Mini-book. ❑ Choose one of the books from the read-aloud suggestions and read it to the students.	❑ Do the "Fingerprint Snakes" activity. ❑ Choose one of the books from the read-aloud suggestions and read it to the students.	❑ Complete the Hands-on Project: Nature Study "Reptiles" and fill out the nature journal sheet.
Supplies Needed for the Week ✓ Day 1: Pictures of reptiles, Peanut butter, Powdered milk, Honey, Cocoa, Vanilla, Chopped Nuts, Raisins, Mini M&M's ✓ Day 2: Thermometer ✓ Day 3: Pictures of reptiles ✓ Day 4: 2 Colors of paint, Paper, Black Marker				

Birds ~ Week 6

Weekly Topic

Main Idea
- Birds have wings and feathers.

Introduction
Have pictures of birds out on the table in front of you. Say to the students:

> **?** *What do you notice about all these animals?*

Give the students time to answer before saying:

> *Those are some good observations! All of these animals are birds. They have wings and feathers that help them fly.*
>
> *This week, we are going to look at birds.*

Student Diary Assignment
- Have the students color the coloring page found on SD pg. 156.

Lapbook Assignment
- Have the students cut out and color the Birds Mini-book on LT pg. 62. You can have them cut out the main idea graphic included and glue it in the interior of the mini-book or you can write a sentence with what they have learned from the week for them on the inside of the mini-book. Once the students are done, have them glue the booklet into the mini-lapbook.

Hands-on Projects

Scientific Demonstration: No Bones About It

In this demonstration, you will help the students to see what the bones of a bird look like.

Materials Needed
- ✓ Clean, cooked chicken bones
- ✓ Chicken skeleton sketch on pg. 192 of the Appendix

Steps to Complete
1. Follow the directions found on *More Mudpies to Magnets* pg. 175.

Student Diary Assignment
- ☐ With the students, fill out the demonstration sheet found on SD pg. 157.

Nature Study: Birds

This week, you will look for the birds found in your area.

Preparation
- ☌ Read the pp. 27-43 in the *Handbook of Nature Study* to learn more about birds.

Outdoor Time
- ☼ Go on a walk and look for birds to observe. Allow the students to observe them and ask any questions they may have. You can use the information you have learned from reading the *Handbook of Nature Study* to answer their questions or to share information about what they are observing.

Student Diary Assignment
- ☐ With the students, fill out the nature journal sheet found on SD pg. 159. The students can sketch what they have seen or you can write down their observations.

Read-Alouds

Optional Encyclopedia Pages
- 📖 *The Usborne Children's Encyclopedia* pp. 64-65 (Bird Life)

Optional Library Books
- 📖 *About Birds: A Guide for Children* by Cathryn Sill and John Sill
- 📖 *Fine Feathered Friends: All About Birds* by Tish Rabe
- 📖 *How Do Birds Find Their Way?* (Let's-Read-and-Find... Science 2) by Roma Gans
- 📖 *The Magic School Bus Flies from the Nest* by Joanna Cole and Carolyn Bracken

Coordinating Activities

These following activities will help you to reinforce the week's topic and main idea.

- ✂ Art – (Feather Painting) Collect feathers from outside or buy feathers from the store. Give the students a sheet of paper and some paint. Have them use the feathers as a paintbrushes to paint a picture.

Student Diary Assignment
- ☐ Have the students use SD pg. 158 to complete this activity.

Lapbook Assignment
- 📁 Have the students add the page they painted to the "My Zoology Projects" pocket in the lapbook.
- ✂ Snack – (Eat like a bird) Explain to the students that many birds eat fruit and seeds. Serve various types of fruits, such as mangoes, blueberries, or strawberries, along with a few sunflower seeds for snack.
- ✂ More Fun – (Backyard Birds) Observe and record (either in a notebook or with photos) the birds you see in your backyard. You may also want to put out a bird feeder so that you attract more birds.

Notes

Possible Schedules for Week 6

Two Days a Week Schedule	
Day 1	Day 2
❑ Read the introduction with the students. Color the main idea page. ❑ Complete the Hands-on Project "No Bones About It" and fill out the demonstration sheet.	❑ Complete the Hands-on Project: Nature Study "Birds" and fill out the nature journal sheet. ❑ Do the "Feather Painting" activity.
Supplies Needed for the Week ✓ Day 1: Pictures of birds, Clean, cooked chicken bones, Chicken skeleton sketch from the Appendix ✓ Day 2: Feathers, Paint, Paper	

Five Days a Week Schedule				
Day 1	Day 2	Day 3	Day 4	Day 5
❑ Read the introduction with the students. Color the main idea page. ❑ Eat like birds for snack.	❑ Complete the Hands-on Project "No Bones About It" and fill out the demonstration sheet. ❑ Read the selected pages in *The Usborne Children's Encyclopedia*.	❑ Have some more fun with the "Backyard Birds" activity. ❑ Complete the Birds Mini-book. ❑ Choose one of the books from the read-aloud suggestions and read it to the students.	❑ Do the "Feather Painting" activity. ❑ Choose one of the books from the read-aloud suggestions and read it to the students.	❑ Complete the Hands-on Project: Nature Study "Birds" and fill out the nature journal sheet.
Supplies Needed for the Week ✓ Day 1: Pictures of birds, Mangoes, Blueberries, or Strawberries, Sunflower seeds ✓ Day 2: Clean, cooked chicken bones, Chicken skeleton sketch from the Appendix ✓ Day 3: Bird feeder ✓ Day 4: Feathers, Paint, Paper				

Intro to Science
Appendix

Rock Candy Recipe

Ingredients

- ✓ Food coloring
- ✓ Glass jars
- ✓ Oven mitts
- ✓ Saucepan
- ✓ Spoons
- ✓ Pencils
- ✓ Paper
- ✓ Binder clips
- ✓ Cotton string
- ✓ 3 Cups Sugar

Steps to Make

1. Begin by boiling about one cup water and add about two cups of sugar.
2. Pour the water into a glass jar and then slowly stir in remaining sugar, about a teaspoon at a time. (*Note—Be careful to not rush this step.*)
3. Continue stirring until the sugar no longer dissolves and starts to collect at the bottom of the jar.
4. Choose a color for your crystals and add a couple of drops of food coloring.
5. Tie one end of a piece of string around the middle of a pencil and tie a paper clip to the other end.
6. Place the pencil over the jar so that the string hangs down and the paper clip almost touches the bottom of the jar.
7. Allow the jar to sit someplace where it will be undisturbed.
8. Check after about 24 to 48 hours, and you'll see colorful crystals forming on the paper clip.
9. Let the solution sit for several weeks and you will have some rock candy to eat!

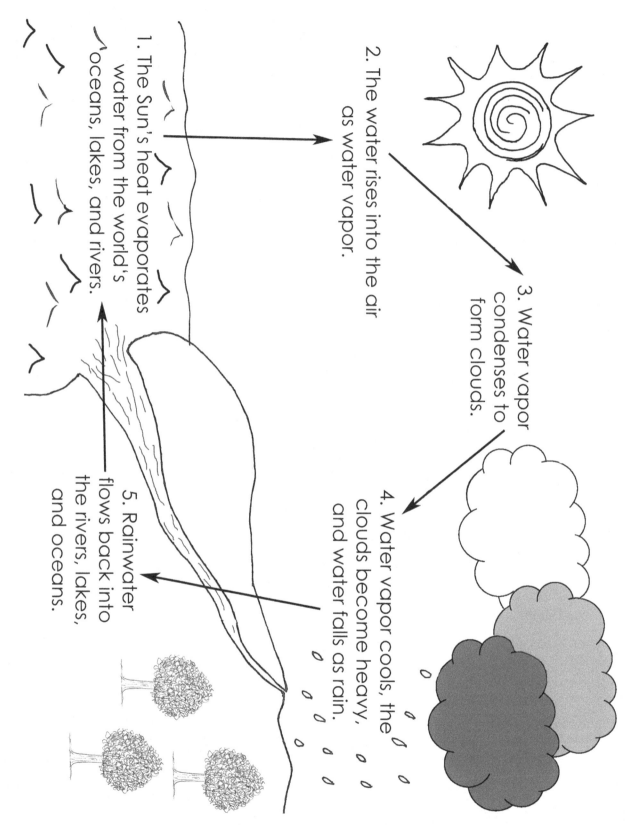

Parts of a Flower

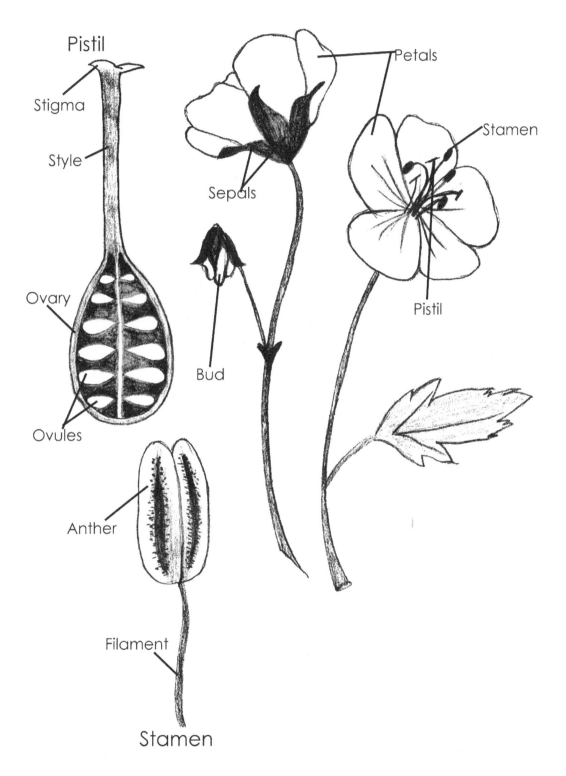

Parts of a Seed

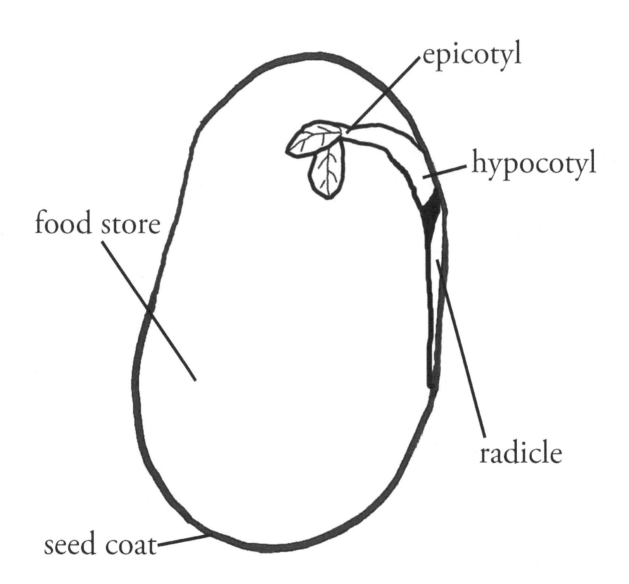

Butterfly Life Cycle Pictures

Butterflies lay eggs on leaves.

Caterpillars hatch out of the eggs and eat the leaves.

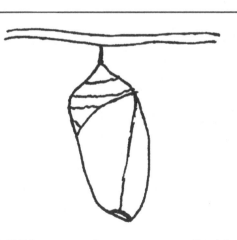

When they are full, caterpillars make a chrysalis.

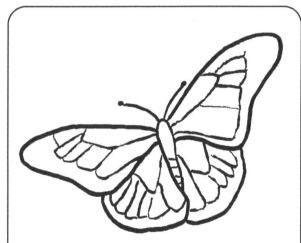

A butterfly emerges from the chrysalis.

Intro to Science Teacher Guide ~ Appendix

Chicken Skeleton

Intro to Science
General Templates

Narration Sheet

Project Record Sheet

> Paste a picture of your project in this box.

What I Learned:

_____
_____
_____
_____
_____
_____
_____

Two Days a Week Schedule

Day 1	Day 2
❏	❏
❏	❏
❏	❏
❏	❏
❏	❏
❏	❏

Things to Prepare

❏

❏

❏

Notes

Five Days a Week Schedule

Day 1	Day 2	Day 3	Day 4	Day 5
☐	☐	☐	☐	☐
☐	☐	☐	☐	☐
☐	☐	☐	☐	☐
☐	☐	☐	☐	☐

All Week Long

☐

☐

Things to Prepare

☐

☐

☐

Notes